# "Menopausal Mommy"
# And Other Essays

*Wit and Wisdom for Women of Any Age*

## by Gretchen Switzer

Booklocker.com, Inc.
2011

This book is dedicated to my family,
who never fails to help me find the humor in life.
I love you more than you will ever know.

Gretchen

"Seize the moment. Remember all those women on the 'Titanic' who waved off the dessert cart."
— Erma Bombeck, Humorist

# Table of Contents

**Preface**

**Motherhood**

| | | |
|---|---|---|
| 1. | Menopausal Mommy | 1 |
| 2. | My Kids Were Nice to Me This Morning! | 4 |
| 3. | Baby Tooth Lost and Found | 8 |
| 4. | Autumn Morning Moments | 11 |
| 5. | A Good Reminder | 12 |
| 6. | The Day I Slept In | 15 |
| 7. | Love You Forever... | 20 |
| 8. | What Was Wrong With the Old Math? | 23 |
| 9. | Have You Ever Had One of Those Mornings? | 25 |
| 10. | Happy Valentine's Day! | 29 |
| 11. | Okay, Okay!  So Disney Is Great! | 31 |
| 12. | Mixed Emotions | 35 |
| 13. | Christmas Eve Perspective | 37 |
| 14. | Puppy Paradise | 39 |
| 15. | We've Adopted A New Family Member Again . . . | 41 |
| 16. | The Flu is Living at Our House! | 44 |

**Middle Age**

| | | |
|---|---|---|
| 17. | Just Received My AARP Card... | 46 |
| 18. | M.I.R.I. | 48 |
| 19. | Sleepless in February | 51 |
| 20. | Laundry, Lunges and Laziness | 54 |
| 21. | You Know You're Middle-Aged When... | 56 |

22.  Never Do Today What You
        Can Put off For 35 Years!                                        58
23.  A Word to the Wise                                                  60
24.  Ahhh! To Feel Young Again!                                          62
25.  A Teacher's Best Lesson                                             64
26.  The Toilet Paper Wars                                               66
27.  God and Menopause: An Eternal Question                             68
28.  Help! I Have a Chess Board on My Face!                             71
29.  Lessons Learned at Middle Age: Part 1                              73
30.  Lessons Learned at Middle Age: Part 2                              75

**The World Today**
31.  Automation Run Amok!                                                79
32.  Me and India:  A Love Affair                                        83
33.  Software and Pumpkin Pie                                            86
34.  Dinner at the Brown Derby                                           89
35.  A Car That Can Park Itself?                                         92
36.  People Give Me The Finger a Lot and
        Other Things That Tick Me Off!                                   94
37.  Too Strange to Be Real                                              99
38.  Today's Televisions Commercials and Me                            102
39.  I Want Your Privacy Back!                                          105
40.  We Now Interrupt Your Regular
        Programming to Bring You This Political Opinion                 108
41.  Twisted                                                            110
42.  THUD!                                                              113
43.  I Had a Nightmare That I Was Sarah Palin (2008)                    115

**Epilogue**                                                           117

# Preface

I heard a wonderful phrase recently: "Age-appropriate mental illness." Age-appropriate mental illness is the craziness that comes to us unbidden at certain times in our lives. It is when a teenager yells, screams and rips her parents to shreds one moment and is tender and loving the next. It is when a man hitting midlife dons a toupee and buys a convertible and tries to wear one while driving the other with the top down. Age-appropriate mental illness is when your lonely old neighbor begins collecting cats.

At some points in our lives, we are all a little crazy. It's a natural part of being human. In order to survive the insanity of life, many of us learn to laugh at ourselves and at other people. We can find humor in almost any situation, and as long as we keep on laughing, we know we will be okay.

If this book helps you find the humor in a challenging situation or brings a smile to your face, if only for a moment, then I have done what I set out to do.

Thanks for sharing a laugh with me!

Gretchen

# Motherhood

# 1. Menopausal Mommy

My friend has waited 25 years to laugh at me raising children. She married right after her college graduation and had two children who are now in college and graduating from college. I waited...

And waited. I went to graduate school and began a career as an ordained United Church of Christ minister while my friend was chasing toddlers around, and driving her children from soccer practice to riding lessons to first jobs. I was dealing with the challenges of being a woman in a traditionally male profession. I was building a solid professional reputation.

I was falling in love, the real thing, in my late twenties.

Dave and I got married when he was 29 and I was 32. We were still building our careers, and once we were ready for children, we chose to adopt. We did the paperwork, underwent the interviews, did the security checks, fingerprints and laser ID's, and then we waited... and waited.

When our daughter, Grace, came off the airplane from South Korea at seven and a half months old, I was 40 years old. I had not changed a diaper since I babysat to earn money in seventh grade. Child number two arrived from Korea 18 months later. Our son, Spencer, was eight months old when we first held him. I was 42.

*I knew parenthood wouldn't be a breeze, but in some ways, I think I figured "How bad could it be?"*

My friend had waited decades to watch me raise children: For years, she had regaled me with tales of how, when the time came, she would sit with her feet up, drinking rum at my kitchen table as she watched me chase those little toddlers around. She would make fun of me as I disposed of poopy diapers and pacifiers. She would taunt me (good-naturedly, of course) while in a few short years, I was going into menopause while Grace was in puberty.

I, of course, found nothing even remotely amusing about this scenario. I knew parenthood wouldn't be a breeze, but in some ways, I think I figured, "How bad could it be?"

Turns out my friend knew many things I did not know. She knew what it was like to try to talk on the phone with two kids scream-ing in your other ear. She knew how it felt to work "through" the throbbing headache to calm down the dog, the children and your spouse all at once and in that order. She comprehended what it might be like for a skunk to spray the dog at midnight when you had to be up at six the next morning to get the kids to school, the trash out and smell good for work. My friend understood that you don't truly "get" what being a mother really is until you become one.

Although my friend has not been drinking at my kitchen table, she has had a few very good and probably satisfying laughs at my expense to keep her going. She has especially enjoyed the stories of baby spit-up on my business suits, trying to get hundreds of tiny little ants out of a backpack, toddlers running up from the pew to hug my knees while I was preaching the Sunday sermon, and find-ing grape jelly sticking my pages together while in the middle of preaching that very same sermon to hundreds of people.

The truth is that while my friend has been guffawing at me, I have been about the business of acquiring many new and useful life skills – I can talk on the telephone, surf the net, mop the floor and clean chocolate off my kids' eyebrows all at the same time. I am learning not to ask "why" before I clean the marshmallow fluff out of my daughter's hair or scrub the marker off the bottom of my son's feet. There is plenty of time to ask "why?" later, like when I am taking the snack bag off the shrub by the front door. Besides, even if they do tell me why, it won't make any sense to me. I am too old and too sensible to fathom why anyone would drop their toothbrush in the toilet to see if it would float!

And anyway, I will probably figure it all out tomorrow when I climb on the garage roof to retrieve the frisbee, the bicycle and the hamster.

# 2. My Kids Were Nice to Me This Morning

This morning has been filled with rare moments, in that it is Sunday, my husband is at work and my children brought me breakfast in bed, complete with a picture of a flower because they were still in their jammies and didn't think it wise to go outside to pick any actual blooms. I knew the breakfast was coming because I could hear the two of them strategizing downstairs about which cereal was my favorite, who would cut the banana and should they attempt to see how the coffeemaker worked. Wisely, they decided against making coffee and explained this apologetically when they brought me my cereal, juice and newspaper.

Then a very strange thing happened. My seven and nine-year-old kids went into one of their rooms to play and left me alone for two hours without pestering me or even fighting with each other. Something was up. The two of them have never played together that long without somebody getting smacked by the other somebody. I read the paper, cleaned up the kitchen (it wasn't too bad) and wrote some letters, but not without a growing sense of suspicion. Clearly, I was being "buttered up" like a Thanksgiving turkey. I was about to be asked to do something to which my kids knew I would be reluctant to agree. They figured I needed persuasion and they needed leverage. Hmmm... Now to figure out what my two little darlings have up their sleeves.

BOOGIE WOOGIE BOWLING!!! That was it. I vaguely recalled saying something in a weak moment when my mind was on something else far more important... I remember agreeing to consider taking them mini-golfing and bowling under the disco ball at Boogie Woogie Lanes! Shoot! That's what all this was about!

And yes, you read it right. Boogie Woogie Bowling... disco ball... It seems that plain old bowling isn't good enough anymore, but these folks had to go and start offering bowling under black lights and a mirrored ball! From a kid's perspective, this is the best idea since chicken fingers and fries. From a parent's point of view, this is the worst idea since one-piece full-body snowsuits that must be removed completely in order to use the toilet. My personal philosophy is that people who come up with ideas like this should be appropriately punished.

The reason I say that is that the last time I took these two to Boogie Woogie Bowling even with regular lighting, we went into the arcade afterward and my son melted down and broke into tiny little emotional pieces as soon as he'd used his last quarter. Mind you, I had not seen a hissy fit like this in my own family since 2002 and I was not pleased. So...

Now we're going to overload them with flashing lights and spinning mirrors and expect them to behave well?

This was my choice at that moment: Let them go on trying to win me over with the best they could give for the rest of the day and make them actually ask to go mini-golfing and bowling, or quietly sneak out of the house and hide behind a rock until their father came home or name what they were doing right to their faces. I, seasoned and clever mother that I am, made the absolute wrong choice.

I was ever so full of myself as I sauntered into the sunroom where they were playing and said, "Ah-hah! I gotcha! I know what all this niceness is about!"

" BOOGIE WOOGIE LANES! BOOGIE WOOGIE LANES!! BOOGIE WOOGIE LANES!!!" they chanted in unison, as if they were at a pep rally.

"Hah! Ha!" I cried, "I knew you were up to something."

Then, as any reasonable, experienced mom would have antici- pated, my seven-year-old son, looked gleefully at his sister and said, "Hey, this is GREAT! She figured it out! We don't have to be nice to her anymore!"

Like I said... wrong choice. For the next two hours, they whined, moped, and generally made them- selves and me miserable, until out of a sheer sense of self-pres- ervation, I agreed that their dad

> *"Hey, this is GREAT! She figured it out! We don't have to be nice to her anymore!"*

and I would take them Boogie Woogie Bowling when their dad got home.

On my own behalf, I have to say that I regrouped pretty well. I pulled myself together and decided to look at this as a nice fam- ily outing, which it was... until...we discovered that what goes with the black lights and the disco ball is blaring music, primar- ily of the disco variety. Now, we are older parents and we are not ashamed, but there is a reason disco was allowed to die. I now know that reason was so we would not have to witness our pumped-up, out-of-control son practicing his dance "gyrations" in the middle of the alley before he threw the ball. And not just at the beginning of each turn, but as he approached the line to throw every single shot.

Just when we thought it couldn't get any worse, my kids heard the next song on the speaker and were off and barking - Yes, that's right - "Who Let the Dogs Out?" Now I know I am showing my age here, but who writes a song called "Who Let the Dogs Out?" and who pays them to sing it? And why is it playing at mega decibels while I'm trying to have my nice family outing?

I regroup again. Just as we get our boy calmed down enough to stop barking, a teenager comes by saying these fateful words to him, complete with a "high five": "You have nice moves, kid!" The dancing, the grunting, the barking began all over again at a furious pace, only this time he's competing with a completely different song on the speaker. We exercised our parental authority (hah!) and canceled the minigolf portion of the evening, but not before we went to the snack bar to get some supper.

We placed our orders. The girl said to sit down and she'd bring us our food. We waited. And waited. And we waited...while she flirted with the young man who had been in line behind us. The music is still blaring, the disco ball is still twirling, our children are still hopped up on loud noises and flashing lights and there we sit. Fifteen minutes later, she comes out not carrying anything and asks if we still want our meal. "Yes," we explained, "we thought that was implied when we placed an order." We waited some more. I don't know what I thought we were waiting for exactly, but the microwave hot dogs and chicken tenders were not good. I mean really not good. As toddlers, my kids had a toy kitchen set that came with a plastic hot dog that fit into an equally plastic bun with a "snap." I can say assuredly that the dogs in their kitchen set were better than these.

The good news was that the day was over. Our children fell blissfully asleep on the way home, and I went to bed after this time with my little dears carrying with me a new take on an old philosophy: "There's no such thing as a free breakfast in bed."

# 3. Baby Tooth Lost and Found

**M**ONDAY AFTERNOON
My seven-year-old came home from school last week carrying a tiny little baby tooth in a Ziploc bag. "Wow," I said, "Did you lose a tooth at school today?"

"Uh...yeah. I guess."

"Well, that's exciting, isn't it! Can I see where it came from?" I said, looking her straight in the mouth...

But, same mouth. Same teeth, all still where they were the last time I looked. Hmmmm.

"Honey, where did you lose that tooth from? Everything looks the same."

"That's because it is the same," she said with a building tone of confession.

"Okay, what's the story, kiddo? Did you lose a tooth or not?"

"Well, no. But Lindsay did!"

Quickly trying to assemble the pieces of the story, I queried, "Okay. So Lindsay lost a tooth at school today?"

"Yes."

"And Lindsay is in your class?"

"No."

"How do you know Lindsay?"

"We played together during recess."

"Is that when she lost her tooth?"

"I dunno. I guess," she responded, waving the plastic bag in the air to see how the tooth moved.

"Look, is that your tooth or somebody else's?" I said, as the true identity of the tooth's owner settled in.

"Somebody else's."

" So, why did Lindsay give you her baby tooth?"

"She didn't. Alicia did."

"So this is Alicia's baby tooth?" I grab the Ziploc from her tiny hands, horrified.

"Of course," my daughter said calmly, as I envisioned a kid on the other side of town melting down at bedtime because she didn't have a tooth to leave under her pillow for the tooth fairy.

"Why did Alicia give you her baby tooth? And where did the plastic bag come from?"

"You sent my snack in it, remember?"

"This is your used snack bag with some other kid's tooth in it?!!!!"

Clearly, Mother was headed for a melt-down.

"It's okay, Mom. She gave it to me."

"Don't you think her parents will wonder where her tooth is when she tells them it fell out?"

> *I envisioned a kid on the other side of town melting down at bedtime because she didn't have a tooth to leave under her pillow for the tooth fairy.*

"Mo-o-om! Her parents already know, okay? Look, Alicia's tooth fell out yesterday. The tooth fairy left her money, but she forgot to take

9

the tooth. Soooo, Alicia brought the tooth in for show and tell and when I said it was cool, she gave it to me."

"Still, honey, that's someone else's tooth!" I exclaimed, imagining a myriad of hygiene and health issues.

"I want to put it under my pillow tonight and see if the tooth fairy will leave me money."

"But it's not your tooth!"

"I don't think the tooth fairy will know the difference."

"Isn't that lying, honey? Besides, isn't your friend going to want her tooth back?"

"Oh, Alicia's not my friend. I never met her until today."


**TUESDAY MORNING**

I attempt to write a note to the teacher:

First draft: *"Dear Mrs. Feingold, enclosed please find a tooth..."*

Second Draft: *"Dear Mrs. Feingold, Grace brought a baby tooth home with her yesterday, but apparently said tooth did not come out of her mouth..."*

Finally: *"Dear Mrs. Feingold, I know that you folks are big on sharing at school, but THIS is ridiculous!"*

# 4. Autumn Morning Moments

Early this morning, the sky outside my window, above the trees, was the color of blueberries and salt water. A tiny, silvery white slice of the moon still hung with no means of suspension. The air was crisp with the refreshment of fall, even though the sun would bring summer-like heat later.

> *. . . beautiful faces I have memorized, newly mature expressions I have yet to fully comprehend, tiny voices that whisper love and laughter into my ear.*

But for one moment, the moon hung and the sky shone and the leaves of the tall trees began to resemble a sunset. For one solitary minute, I gazed out the window and just appreciated creation, for I knew I might not do that again all day.

Early this morning, two children crawled into my bed and snuggled against me under the covers - a girl and a boy, about to get ready for elementary school – beautiful faces I have memorized, newly mature expressions I have yet to fully comprehend, tiny voices that whisper love and laughter into my ear. Later today, the same voices will be yelling at each other about who asked first or to whom it belongs. They will ring through the house in defiance until they are calmed and hushed by lullabies and bedtime stories. Then they will drift off to sleep.

Nevertheless, for one moment this morning, two sets of bright, wide-open, sparkling eyes looked into mine, and tiny voices whispered love and laughter and I gazed back. I appreciated and was grateful and thanked God because I knew I might not do that again all day.

# 5. A Good Reminder

The other day, I found a mini GI Joe in the garbage disposal... after I had crushed him to smithereens. This was especially interesting because we don't allow our son to play with weapons or war toys, leading me to the conclusion that I had just obliterated the favorite toy of one of the other kids in the neighborhood.

My kids came home from school and I asked my son whose GI Joe it was that I had destroyed in the garbage disposal. "Moooaaaahm! You killed GI Joe? M-ahhhhhh-m! That wasn't even ours! How could you do that?"

"How could I do that? I didn't know there was a GI Joe in the garbage disposal. It never occurred to me to look. How could I have known there was a toy soldier in there when there isn't even supposed to be one in the house? Who did it belong to anyway?"

"Jerry," my son said sadly.

"Well, honey, I'm sure a little boy like Jerry has a lot of toys and if we have to, we'll replace the one you put in the disposal."

"Gerry's a girl!" laughed my daughter, Grace.

"Yeah, Mom, Gerry's a girl." Spencer chimed in, finally calming down. I envisioned a traditional "tomboy" with skinned knees, worn blue jeans and a somewhat masculine swagger.

"Oh. Well, where does Gerry live?"

"I don't know, but she was visiting Tommy next door. She's his cousin or something. She had the biggest collection of GI Joes I've ever seen!"

"Well, you'll just have to explain to her what happened and apologize and offer to buy her a new one with your own money."

"Ah, Mom, but I've been saving up for that cool solar system!"

"Your own money, Spence. You put him in the garbage disposal."

"O-kaaaay. I'll go talk to her now."

"Good job," I exclaimed and went on with my chores around the house. Ten minutes later, the doorbell rang, and when I opened the door I found standing before me the prettiest, most feminine little girl I had ever seen.

"Hello, Mrs. James. Spencer told me what happened and I came to see if there were any pieces left to my GI Joe. I want to see if I can kinda put him back together. He's my favorite one."

I was taken aback by my own expectations. When my kids told me that Gerry was a girl who had a GI Joe collection, I had made a certain set of unfounded assumptions, but here I was standing at my door discussing GI Joe body parts with a delicate flower, all dressed up in a party dress, with a sash, an embroidered bodice, lace-topped bobbie socks and

*She explained to me that you can have a manicure and still throw a football and you can enjoy boys' company without being "in looooove" with one.*

patent leather shoes (I didn't even know they made those any-more!). She even had ribbons in her hair!

I chatted with Gerry for awhile on our front steps and discovered she had a better handle on who she was than most grown women do. At age 8½, being feminine and enjoying traditional "boys" play were not incompatible in her mind. To her, it was all just part of who she was and even better, who she wanted to be. She told me that there was nothing boys do that girls couldn't do. She explained to me that you can have a manicure and still throw a football and you can enjoy boys' company without being "in looooove" with one.

I couldn't help but think that this is a much healthier way to grow up than thinking that boys' and girls' interests and gifts are mutually exclusive. I would bet that this little girl will soon be a woman who can do anything she sets her mind to, while being true to herself. If she marries, she will have the good sense to fall in love with a man who appreciates all of who she is and what that means, a man who will respect and honor her as an individual, and with whom she can work as a team to create a great life together.

Gerry, I am deeply sorry I crushed your GI Joe, but meeting you was an inspiration and a reminder that no matter what gender we are, we are most happy when we are uniquely and genuinely ourselves. And Gerry – you go, girl!

# 6. The Day I Slept In

I have had the flu for a week, and yet every morning I have dragged myself out of bed and gotten the children off to school. Then I have come home and collapsed until it was time to drag myself out of the house yet again to pick the children up from school. After bringing them home, I have dropped myself back into bed and prayed for the assistance of my husband, who arrives home in the late afternoon.

This weekend was all I was living for. My hubby was off work Saturday and Sunday and I could kind of take it easy. Over all, this worked out extremely well, but then Sunday morning arrived. We had decided not to go to church and to sleep in as long as we wanted. "We" however, only applied to Dave and me! Quite out of the ordinary, the children picked this morning to awaken energized at 6:30 a.m. They played together nicely for awhile, they even got themselves breakfast and kept the arguing to a minimum, but at 7:06 a.m, our darling children decided we should be awake and out of bed. Thus began "The Sunday Morning Torture Hour."

I first awakened to my daughter screaming at the top of her lungs, right next to my ear, "WAKE UP! It's time for you to get up, Mummy. We'll be late!"

"Late? What?" My head sprang off the pillow. Late for what? It's Sunday right? Not going to church, right? My head is spinning from flu and confusion, I come to, suddenly look my beautiful daughter in the eye and ask, "What am I late for? It's Sunday."

"Oh, yeah," she says sheepishly backing away from our bed, "I forgot."

I look at the clock, **7:13 a.m.** – I'll go back to sleep.

**Fifteen minutes later:**

I hear the door to our bedroom squeak and whoosh against the carpet as our son tiptoes in. "Mom," he whispers. "Mom," he whispers again. I pretend not hear him, the same way I pretended not to hear my mother when I was kid and she was waking me up for school. "Mom, I think you should get up now."

"Why?" I asked muffled by the cozy warmth of my pillow.

"Because... because I'm bored."

"Go find yourself something to do. Build a robot or (yeah, here's a thought) read a book. I'm trying to sleep in!" My son leaves in a huff.

I look at the clock, **7:31 a.m.** It's the weekend – I'll go back to sleep.

**7:34 a.m.** Our bedroom door opens suddenly and a cold, wet dog is encouraged by our daughter, Grace, to jump on top of us in our bed, which of course, she does. And in case that didn't disturb our sleep, Gracie slams our bedroom door as hard as she can after letting the dog in the room.

I look at the clock, **7:38 a.m.** I've been sick. I'll go back to sleep.

I am just approaching REM again when I feel a finger touching my right eyelid. I am too tired to even move, as the small digit lifts the lid to reveal my very sleepy eye. Holding my eye open, my son says softly, "Mom? You asleep, Mom?"

"Of course I'm not asleep! You are holding my eye wide open!"

"Oh," he says, "So you were awake."

"No, I was asleep, with both eyes closed because I am sleeping in!"

"But you were snoring, Mom. I thought I'd better wake you up."

"Why? Was my snoring bothering you?"

"Yes."

"Where were you?"

"Down in the TV room."

"Spencer, are you saying you could hear my snoring on the first floor on the other side of the whole house?"

"No, I just heard it when I came upstairs to get something."

*I am just approaching REM again, when I feel a finger touching my right eyelid. I am too tired to even move, as the small digit lifts the lid to reveal my very sleepy eye. Holding my eye open, my son's says softly, "Mom? You asleep, Mom?"*

"So, you are going back downstairs where it will not bother you because you won't be able to hear it?"

"Yeah, I guess."

"So, you woke me up again because..."

"I just thought you would want to know."

"That I was snoring?"

"Yeah, I'm glad you're awake now. " And now, he slips quietly out of the room.

I look at the clock. It's **8:02 a.m**. I am going back to sleep.

By then, I was so irritated and so angry that I lay in bed fuming. But after a few hard-hitting tosses and turns, I eventually fall back to sleep.

**8:20 a.m.**

"Mom! Mom! Mom, can I use the computer?" A small hand grabs my shoulder and shakes.

" Yeah , but only for the twenty minutes you're allowed."

"Thanks, Mom."

**8:23 a.m.**

"Mom! Mom!" (it's the other kid) "Mom, can I watch TV?"

"Yeah," I grumble sleepily.

That should do it, I think to myself, as I snuggle back under the blanket.

18

Ten minutes later World War Three erupts downstairs. The kids are screaming, the dog is barking. I stumble down half-asleep, and manage to inquire (quite loudly) "What the hell is going on down here?" After hearing two completely different explanations at exactly the same time and punishing both of them, I stomp back up to my bed, realizing with each step that the flu from earlier in the week is not completely done with me.

I literally crawl up the stairs and drop myself into bed, but just as I drift off again, I feel my husband stir beside me. "Wow," he says, not realizing it's the last sentence he will ever speak, "Wasn't it nice to sleep in this late undisturbed?"

# 7. Love You Forever ...

**I**sn't time a mystery? It seems to me that of all the things we can explain through science and through faith, the one thing we human beings cannot control, cannot even influence, is the passage of time.

Surely that is what Ponce de Leon was hoping to do when he sought the proverbial "Fountain of Youth." Even our own American obsession with daylight savings time is a pathetic attempt to control what we so clearly cannot.

Time is bewildering. Even as I sit at my computer and record these thoughts, even as you sit at your desk or in your favorite comfy chair to read them, time is passing at an alarming rate. Our new car has lost thousands of dollars in value in the split second it took to drive it out of the dealer's lot. Our daughters, just yesterday in diapers and onesies, are suddenly in the throes of pre-adolescent angst, while we whose bodies would "never get that old" are sagging and bagging in all the wrong places, and our own hormones are dancing a lively version of the Cha-cha-cha. Seems like only a few weeks ago when we were dreaming of getting married to prince charming and having wonderfully perfect children, but now? Now the subjects my husband and I most recently discussed were long term care insurance and living wills.

My mother used to tell me that she couldn't understand how aging worked or how time changed us. "I'm the same person inside that I was at eighteen," she would remark. "I know I don't look like that and I know I don't move like that, but inside me, in the place where I am me, I have the same dreams, the same hopes, the same passions that I felt at eighteen."

I didn't truly understand what she meant back then. I was 18 at the time. Now, that I'm on the brink of 50, her words are slipping into perspective. It is true that I am heavier, slower and most certainly not as pretty as I was then, but inside, in the place that makes me me, I am hopeful, excited and more than a little apprehensive about life and time. There, I am still fall-

*Seems like only a few weeks ago when we were dreaming of getting married to prince charming and having wonderfully perfect children, but now? Now the subjects my husband and I most recently discussed were long term care insurance and living wills.*

ing in love for the very first time, and daydreaming wistfully about my love sweeping me up in his arms and carrying me away on his white charger. In the deepest reaches of my being, I am still curious about what the years ahead will bring, and when I allow myself the room to do so, even catch myself daydreaming about how many wonderful things could come to pass in my life between now and the end of it. The young girl who dreamt of fame and love is still there inside me. The only difference is that I no longer believe in the possibilities of what can happen. Time has made me realistic in the sad sort of way I used to berate my parents for. I know now that I will never be an opera singer (age two), or world-famous figure skater (age 11). I will not go on world singing tours with my guitar and write music for a living (ages 14-25), nor will I rock humanity with my ideas on achieving world peace or be called to the Oval Office to tutor a U.S. president on conflict resolution (in my 30s and 40s). The dreams have changed with the passage of time, and I grieve the loss of some of them very deeply. Truth is, though, that I still dream and I still have wishes to fulfill. The truth also is that my life is far better than it would have been if any of those dreams I dreamt when I was younger had come true.

I realized that last night when I went to a beautiful concert and sat in the darkened theater holding hands with my husband. And I realized it when I collected a message my seven-year-old son left for me while I was at that concert. He waited patiently for the beep on the voice mail, and said, "Mom. I love you. I'm missing you tonight," and then right there on that voice mail message he broke into what has been "our song" since he was little, and he sang with such passion and such love in a tiny little just developing singing voice, "Love you forever and forever, Love you with all my heart. Love you whenever we're together. Love you when we're apart..."*And I cried, and I knew it was the most beautiful sound I had ever heard. I also knew I could never have dreamt up anything as moving or meaningful or soul-nurturing at 18 or 49.

Sooner than I think, my son will be a sullen teen, a cocky driver and ultimately a delightful and loving man, but no matter how much time passes, I will remember the night time stopped, if just for a few moments, "Love you forever and forever. Love you with all my heart. Love you whenever we're together, I love you when we're apart..."*

* Beatles song: "I Will"

22

# 8. What Was Wrong With the Old Math?

I can still hear my mother asking that very question 40 years ago when the so-called new math was being taught in schools. As a child at the time, I knew nothing whatsoever about any kind of math. Old math, new math, elderly math, peanut butter math -- it was all the same to me. Frankly, as long as I could count my allowance and make sure I wasn't getting gypped, I simply didn't care what kind of math it was. The truth is that everything comes back to haunt you when you're a parent, and math, apparently, is no exception.

My kids are learning to add the wrong way. Well, maybe not the wrong way – they do get the right answers, but they are not learning to add the way their dad and I learned to add. And I resent that. "What was wrong with adding from the right to the left?" I query my husband. "Our way worked perfectly well. Why can't they leave well enough alone?" I whine, my mother's voice coming out of my mouth. (Aarrggghh!)

> *The truth is that everything comes back to haunt you when you're a parent and math, apparently, is no exception.*

(Now I get what she and my dad were so aggravated about!)

Here I sit staunchly in middle age having to learn how to do math a whole new way so I can help the kids with their homework. Help, by the way, that they don't necessarily want!

Learning this new way of thinking is harder than you might think. Hopeful, I wander into my daughter's second grade class at the end of school one day and say, "Please, teacher, would you teach me how to add?"

The teacher is very kind and understanding. Much to her credit, she doesn't even laugh at me. She takes me to the chalkboard and explains carefully that our children are now learning to add from the left. When adding three-digit numbers, for instance, we add the numbers in the hundreds spot first, then the number in the tens spot and then the ones, so basically, 20 is no longer 20, it is 2 tens and zero ones. Thirty-six is no longer 36, it is three tens and six ones.

HOGWASH! The kids are on their own. I have made my decision. When it comes to addition, change is unnecessary.

STILL, this week, my daughter came home with the niftiest multiplication system I have ever seen – a system that is making it possible for my child to multiply large numbers with no problem at all. ("This," I think to myself, "I should be paying attention to.") My nine-year-old proceeds to teach me how to use the "lattice method" for multiplication. I did it a few times, easily and successfully, and have to admit that it is faster and more accurate than traditional multiplication. If I had been taught this strategy when I was in school, I actually might have liked mathematics!

So, I've learned my lesson. Maybe there are new things under the sun that I have never dreamt of and maybe, just maybe, some of them are good. Perhaps change isn't always a bad thing. Could I learn to be a little more open-minded?

Sure. As long as I can still put two and two together the way I want!

# 9. Have You Ever Had One of Those Mornings?

I know you will think I am making this up, but I can't help that. In spite of four different alarms going off every 15 minutes between 6 a.m. and 7 a.m., I overslept and finally got myself out of bed at 7:30 a.m. I raced down the stairs to start the coffee, only to realize, as I rushed through the living room that someone had let the dog out of her crate and not put her outside. I know this because I step in a little morning gift she leaves on the living room floor - a gift I step in with my barefeet! I hobble quickly and carefully to the paper towels in the kitchen as the gross substance squishes between my toes. I call the dog monstrous, but well-deserved names as I clean my foot with dishwashing soap.

I let the dog out, wondering what the point is since she has already done her morning business on my nice carpet! I grab what I need and go into the living room to clean up the mess.

Once that is done, I refocus on my intended task and go to the coffeemaker. I fill the pot with water from the tap, and begin to pour it into the back of my coffee maker, only to watch half of it spill down the outside of the carafe. For some reason, this happens to me frequently, but this time the water splashes down between the counter and the refrigerator and seeps down underneath the coffeemaker itself. I clean it up, wondering what the rest of the day holds in store. I finally get the coffee bag out of the cabinet and dip my scoop into it, but as I pull the scoop out to put the grounds in the filter basket, my hand slips and about a half a cup of ground coffee spills on the kitchen floor. It lands of course, where the floor is still damp from the water spill and it begins to make cold coffee on my white linoleum. Oh help! I reach for the paper towels, only to realize I left them in the living room when I was cleaning up after the dog. But there is a sponge nearby, I grab it to pick up the coffee grounds, but don't realize until it has made contact with the floor, that this was the sponge one of the kids used to clean up peanut butter off the computer desk the night before. Of course, that individual had not rinsed the PB out of the sponge, so the result by now is a lovely and enticing mixture of un-brewed coffee grounds, grungy sponge, and day-old peanut butter on my formerly clean kitchen floor!

Eventually, I get the coffee made, pour myself a cup and take it upstairs to drink after a quick shower.

I start up the shower and climb in for a quick wash and shampoo, only to find that there is no soap. I step out to the supply basket across the bathroom, I retrieve a new bar of soap and step back into the shower. I set the soap down in its dish and reach for the new shampoo I had bought when I went grocery shopping. A large bottle. A heavy bottle. And for what's it's worth, a blue bottle. I grab it with fingers still slippery from getting the new soap, but it escapes my grasp, landing squarely on my little toe, leaving me wondering if one can actually break a bone by dropping a bottle of shampoo on one's foot. What I fail to notice right away is that the tumble caused the lid of the shampoo to open, covering the tub in which I was taking my shower with a slippery, oddly purplish glaze, which is especially hard to avoid while I am dancing around on one foot and holding my little toe on the other. But I do it. I jump right out of that tub, taking the shower curtain with me, the pressurized shower curtain rod landing squarely on my head.

So there I lie, kind of sprawled across the bathroom with the curtain and rod on top of me, the water still running, my toe still stinging and there's a frantic knock at the door. "Mom! Mom!"

"Yes, honey I'm okay. "

> *So there I lie, kind of sprawled across the bathroom with the curtain and rod on top of me, the water still running, my toe still stinging and there's a frantic knock at the door. "Mom! Mom!"*

"No, Mom. It's not that. I have to use the bathroom right now!"

"Sorry, honey, you'll have to go downstairs."

"NO, Mom! I don't want to go downstairs. I want to use THIS BATHROOM!!!"

"Spencer, I have just jumped out of the tub to avoid the shampoo spill, after having broken my toe, cleaned up coffee grounds with peanut butter and stepped in dog poop with my bare feet. I am now lying on the bathroom floor wearing the shower curtain. Now tell me, which bathroom are you going to use?"

"I'll wait" says he.

"Why can't you just go downstairs and let me figure this morning out here by myself without being rushed?"

"But Mom, I like this toilet better."

"Honey, the toilets in both bathrooms are exactly the same! I know. I bought them!"

"I dunno. I just go to the bathroom better up here."

My head is so near to exploding that I probably should call the bomb squad, and all the while, I am struggling to extricate myself from the shower curtain, get up and turn the shower off. My patience and my sanity are on the endangered list. "Spence, look, you can't use this bathroom right now. If you've gotta go, you must use the bathroom DOWNSTAIRS!"

"Okay, Mom, but it won't be the same," he pouts, as I hear him thump dejectedly down the stairs.

Finally, I am up on my two feet. I have shut the water off. I am rehanging the shower curtain and rod. I may not be clean, but I am soaking wet. I may not be shampooed, and school may have started ten minutes ago, but as far as my son is concerned, I am in the best bathroom with the best toilet and I am going to enjoy it while I can!

# 10. Happy Valentine's Day!!!!

Valentine's Day, 2008. I was encouraged to find that Valentine's Day in the fourth grade is just as big a deal as Valentine's Day in the younger grades. The new and early maturity of nine- and ten-year-olds led me to believe that they might feel they are "above" the Valentine's Day thing, but happily, I was wrong.

Sadly, my fourth grader, Grace, is sick today and missing the Valentine's festivities, but I had promised to bring in stuff for "the party," and so I took her Valentines in to her class myself. I was "tickled" to see all those little kids in the school, rushing inside with their arms overflowing with carefully printed Valentines for their friends and a big red foil box of chocolates for their teacher. It was sweet and it reminded me that even though the kids now seem to be growing up faster, even though they know things about life I didn't know until I was 25, and even though so many of them seem jaded by divided families, terrorism, and violent TV and games, inside they are still just the same little kids we were – trying to figure out the world around them and their place in it, feeling validated and encouraged that someone remembered to put their name on a little red and pink valentine. As "cool" as some of these kids would like us to believe they are, they still need affirmation and encouragement. They still get the same thrill out of sliding down a good snowy hill on a sled until they're so cold

> . . . inside they are still just the same little kids we were - trying to figure out the world around them and their place in it, feeling validated and encouraged that someone remembered to put their name on a little red and pink valentine.

they cant't feel their noses, and they love sitting by a fire later, drinking the same hot chocolate my mother made for us for years.

I sometimes watch the news and grieve the children's loss of innocence, but then, every once in a while, I see a kid carrying an armful of valentines, or crawling into my lap for a hug, and I am reminded that even though the world seems wilder and scarier than it once was, children are still children. They remind us to look for the good in life. They help us recall that sometimes the greatest gifts of all come in the tiny little snippets of life that we adults seem so often not to notice. Children still believe in miracles, and they remind us to be filled with hope for our lives and for the world. Perhaps the innocence of childhood is better hidden these days, but I am happy to report it is not lost!

# 11. Okay, Okay! So Disney Is Great!

There is nothing in all the world so distasteful to me as having to admit that I am wrong. Publicly "eating crow" is just not my style. HOWEVER, Disney was spectacular!

On our first day there, I realized that what I have always disliked about amusement parks is that most of them are dirty - trash on the ground, sticky pathways, ice cream slimed on the sides of trash barrels and disgusting bathrooms. But Disney World is immaculate. Trash is picked up almost before it hits the ground; they go around the theme parks with trash vacuums that suck up every foreign object from the walkways, the shiny things are being shined, the not so shiny things are being washed, the bathrooms are nearly perfect, especially considering there are thousands of people tromping through them everyday! And every-where you look there is someone ready and willing to answer your questions no matter how stupid. The Park employees are pleasant, polite and well dressed, and never make you feel like helping you is an imposition. It is very impressive!

The only real downside I could find at Disney was having to rub elbows with so many other families. Now I have to say that our children were remarkably well-behaved (possibly because they had the threat of losing Disney Dollars for bad behavior hanging over their heads), but this was not so for a large percentage of our fellow park-goers. We noticed a pattern of parental and child behaviors while we were there.

The first behavior I call the "See how quickly we can suck Mommy and Daddy dry" style. These parents could be spotted at the end of just one or two days on vacation looking whipped, for lack of a better description. The parents were working together,

> *This method involves an intense commitment to whining, and the ability to throw oneself down on the floor or pavement in front of as many people as possible and have a hissy fit worthy of an Academy Award. . .*

but the kids were too. They had ganged up on Mom and Dad so quickly and so completely that the grown-ups didn't quite know what had hit them. They did everything but give the children their wallets and let 'em go to town, just to get their offspring off their backs.

The second behavior is one that every parent who ever took their children anywhere has experienced – only kind of larger than life, like Mickey's ears. This style I call "How badly must I humiliate my folks before they give in?" This method involves an intense commitment to whining, and the ability to throw oneself down on the floor or pavement in front of as many people as possible and have a hissy fit worthy of an Academy Award. In this case, Mom and Dad have three options:

A) buying Johnny what he's screaming for (stops the tantrum, but leaves parents sucked into those behaviors for no less than 18 years);

B) getting down on hands and knees and attempting to reason with a kicking, screaming facsimile of that usually nice and amiable child (on the face of it, a good approach, except that no one should negotiate with terrorists, old or young);

C) walk away to a place where you can see your child is safe, but he/she cannot see you, and wait for them to realize you are not honoring their fuss with your attention. (I find that the effect of this tactic is long-lasting, and the child in question may actually skip the tantrum at the next two or three opportunities, but

32

will eventually try it again just in case it was a fluke. This method also leaves you hiding from your child no less than six hours per day.)

A surprising percentage of parents at Disney World choose Option A. Then you keep seeing the same families everywhere you go with Mom and Dad balancing a tower of packages representing at least one purchase each from every gift shop in the Park.

Those who select Option B generally look shell-shocked most of the day. They often have scratch marks on their faces from their insolent toddler's finger nails, or footprints on their backs from the number of other tourists who chose to step on them rather than around them while they were crouched down playing diplomat with their child.

You can always tell the families where Option C has been chosen because the parents generally look relatively relaxed. The whole family seems to be enjoying themselves and each other. These families are even occasionally seen laughing together and are often followed by one or two profusely apologetic little kids. This, I call the "You're Not in Charge, I am" style.

The third behavior is the "If I ignore them, they'll go away" style. This behavior, practiced mostly by dads who don't spend much time with their kids, involves walking down the main street of the Magic Kingdom with a broad gait as if they are there visiting Cinderella all by themselves, while the other parent is fumbling with the little one climbing out of the stroller, dropping their sippy cups in front of unsuspecting strangers and dealing with the teenager who is complaining that he can't hear his girlfriend on his cell phone 1000 miles from home because the park is too noisy. And still, Dad walks along, feeling like the proud leader of the pack, completely unaware of the chaos ensuing directly behind him.

The nice thing about Disney is that nearly everyone who visits there is prepared for all this. Disney visitors understand that the place is built for children. They expect to see adorable, pleasing children and ill-behaved children and to give them a wide berth as they stroll down Sunset Boulevard at Hollywood Studios. Most visitors also anticipate seeing adorable, pleasing parents who have it pretty much together, as well as ill-behaved parents whose children reflect the parents' inability to cope. But it's Disney World, and visitors go there knowing that children will be children and parents will be parents. Together, the community created by the "Happiest Place on Earth" amazingly accepts it all and moves on.

# 12. Mixed Emotions

In 17 days, Grace will turn 10. While in previous generations, this was simply a turning from one to two digits; the modern era has brought with it the early onset of hormonal insanity and pre-teen angst that declares the passage of a girl into her "tweenage" years a monumental life event.

Personally, I am having a little trouble with this because I am about to set sail on a whole new phase of my own life that I consider truly monumental – in 18 days, I will turn 50.

The good news is that most of my own hormonal insanity seems to be behind me and I have now embarked anew on life's journey as a "post-menopausal woman." The troubling thing is that the pundits recounting the Super-duper Tuesday primaries seem to feel that the women's vote essentially split along the lines of peri-menopausal, mid-menopausal and the "all done with that crap" ages. In practically every ounce of the pundits gabbing, a woman of my age became consequential only in that most of us who are Democrats seem to want a woman to ascend to the presidency. That means that once we get a woman in the White House, we may become a completely insignificant constituency with virtually no political influence on anything but Medicare and Social Security!

*This is when I begin to realize that people should really be younger than I am when they have children. I say that because my poor old heart cannot take the idea of my little girl out by herself in a car, much less with a boy!*

My nearly ten-year-old daughter will be old enough to vote and take up arms for our country in eight years. Worse yet, she will have her driver's license in six. She is already asking about when she may have her ears pierced and at what age she might venture out on a date.

This is when I begin to realize that people should really be younger than I am when they have children. I say that because my poor old heart cannot take the idea of my little girl out by herself in a car, much less with a boy!

Old as Grace imagines me to be, I still remember getting my ears pierced; I still recall bringing home a boy with a Mohawk (utterly shocking in 1972); I recall ignoring my homework and spending hours at a time on the telephone with that very same boy. I recall every fiber of my being worrying and feeling proud all at the same time when that young man joined the army; I still remember how it felt when our lives forked off in different directions, but also how much joy it gives me that in midlife we have rediscovered the friendship that first brought us together. All the same, adolescence is such a period of mixed emotions and confusing events that imagining my own kids going through it shakes me to the core. How will they fare out there in that big world? Will they remember that home is only a hug away? Will I know when to hang on, and more important, when to let go? Will they?

This is the best news: I am turning 50. I am way past my own teenage drama; I have survived the loss of friends and forged newer, deeper alliances than I was capable of 30 years ago. I have lived through the challenges and disappointments that were part of a first career, and I am off on a newer adventure that feeds my soul and makes me happy. I have loved my parents through the years and I have survived the immense pain of their deaths. All I can do now is pray that someday, my Grace will grow to be 50 and look back as I do, on a lifetime of love, accomplishment and joy. But for now, she'll have to start by turning ten.

# 13. Christmas Eve Perspective

The weeks and days leading up to Christmas Eve had been hectic for the whole family. My husband, the chef, was working extra hours. There were school shows and church pageant rehearsals and Tae Kwon Do celebrations. By Christmas Eve Day, when my sister arrived, we were all beyond exhausted. Even so, I had cleaned the house enough to have company without being terribly embarrassed and all of us were dressed appropriately and ready to leave on time for our church's Family Christmas Eve Service at 5:30 p.m.

*It is not about the presents or the meals or the Christmas cookies or decorations that we get so caught up in. It's about that quiet, anticipated moment out of time when we realize that we are loved beyond measure forever.*

That year, the service revolved around the children's Christmas Pageant, which had been snowed out two Sundays before. My son, Spencer, was going to play an angel and my daughter, Grace, would be a modern-day gift bearer near the end of the pageant. I had no part in any of it except to deliver my kids on time...but, as I dropped off the kids at the costuming room, I literally bumped into an unusually frantic woman who happened to be the minister of our church. When I inquired if she was okay, she said only, "We've lost a wise man, where is your husband?"

"He's on his way, but I don't know what time he'll arrive." Then without really thinking it through, I blurted out, "Will I do?" And with that I was whisked away to the grown-up costume room, dressed in king's clothing and given the metal container that represented the myrrh the kings brought to the baby Jesus. The next thing I knew, I was sitting in the pew in the darkened sanctuary with an antsy eight-year-old angel at my side. And at his side, his sister sitting there calmly in her Christmas best. When my husband arrived at 5:25, he was surprised to find me in costume, too. I felt unsure of myself, and not quite certain when or where I was to go. I was nervous I would screw it up. We sat there enjoying the organ music, "Are you nervous?" I inquired of my son.

"A little," he said as he grabbed my hand in his. Unexpectedly, the organ music suddenly went from loud proclamation to a quiet, tender version of "Away in a Manger." Spencer looked at me. "Think of it, Mom! Jesus' Spirit is almost here!" His smile was angelic!

In the twinkle of Santa's eye, my soul quieted. All the preparations we had made for the last month were about this, this very moment. The moment when Jesus comes, when God reaches down to touch us in the depths of our being. It is not about the presents or the meals or the Christmas cookies or decorations that we get so caught up in. It's about that quiet, anticipated moment out of time when we realize that we are loved beyond measure forever. We were touched by God that night in new and wonderful ways, and I thanked God my little child led me to the PEACE of the Season.

# 14. Puppy Paradise

Okay, so about eight weeks ago, I took leave of my senses. I suggested, with no prompting from anyone, that perhaps our 9 ½-year-old son might enjoy a dog for whom he could take responsibility. I also reasoned aloud that Sophia, our Sheltie, who is the primadonna-est of primadonnas, might benefit from some canine companionship. To have another doggie in the house, we hoped, would bring her down a notch or two from her high perch in the land of the spoiled!

These were the limitations on my idea: no puppies. Dogs under one year old would not be considered; any animal coming into our home would have to already be reliably housetrained; we would try to get a rescue or a shelter dog, rather than buy from a breeder. The new dog would have to be small like Sophia; no yappy dogs; everyone in the family would have to meet the dog before we considered bringing it home. Spencer would be responsible for feeding, walking and grooming the new dog. This was my plan and I was sticking to it!

*. . . running through my head were romanticized scenes of a little coton puppy jumping all over my son and daughter and giving them sloppy kisses while they laughed hysterically.*

I scoured the internet for rescue dogs, shelter dogs. We checked out Portuguese Water Dogs like "Bo" Obama out of affection and respect for our president. Every day, I searched for an hour or more in hopes of discovering that there was a dog waiting for us who needed a family, but no one was just right.

A few weeks later, we were out hiking and met the prettiest

little dog we'd ever seen. Her owner told us she was a rare breed called a "Coton De Tulear." When I googled the breed, I discovered that "Cotons" were originally lap dogs to royalty in the port town of Tulear, located in Madagascar. The pho-

*The picture in my imagination was intoxicating.*

tos were cute, and running through my head were romanticized scenes of a little coton puppy jumping all over my son and daughter and giving them sloppy kisses while they laughed hysterically. The picture in my imagination was intoxicating, of course, and after contacting several Coton breeders, checking references and researching the breed, my husband and I decided this was the dog for us. Nevermind that she was everything we did not plan on when this brainchild began. She was cute, she was small and she was trained to a doggy door. How bad could it be? (Oops! There I go again.)

Today is Friday, May 8. Tonight, we drive to the airport to pick up a four-month-old puppy named "Aruba," whom we have never met before. She was born eight hours away. The entire family, including the son for whom the dog was originally considered, has left me with the job of preparing the house for puppy, and as for being "yappy," I guess we'll know by Monday! All this, and only myself to blame!

I feel certain we will need your prayers for the beginning of this journey. She should at least give me tons of blogging material for a while.

# 15. We Have Adopted a New Family Member Again... But This Time It Was Harder!

Soooo, the puppy arrived home ten days ago. We fell in love with her the moment we met, but I have a burning question: In these days of security and caution, why did we have to jump through more hoops to bring a dog home from New York state than we did to bring our children home from South Korea? Granted the initial paperwork was much greater before Grace and Spencer flew halfway around the world, but when they each came off the plane in Chicago, all we did was sign a piece of paper and their escorts handed 'em over. No one ever even looked at our identification to make certain they were giving these children to the right people for the rest of their lives. There we stood holding a baby we had never met, not knowing what to do with her (and two years later, him). My brother-in-law had to show me how to do the classic "baby-bounce" that (supposedly) stopped babies from crying. (In Grace's case not so much.) Our daughter peed on me in the airport bathroom while I was trying, from my teenage babysitting days, to recall how one changes a diaper – (ha! they didn't ask that one on the adoption application, did they?)

Eleven years later, enter a beautiful puppy somewhat the worse for the wear of traveling. First of all, our precious pup got bounced off the originally planned flight because the origi-

> *I was trying, from my teenage babysitting days to recall how one changes a diaper - (ha! they didn't ask that one on the adoption application, did they?)*

nally planned airline got a better offer. A whole kennel of dogs from Europe bought tickets to get to a dog show in Providence, RI, so they bumped our new friend and we all had to scramble to rearrange the plan. Presumably, the airline opted for this course of action because an entire kennel's worth of dogs meant more money.

Everything rearranged, we head to the airport with our son to meet "Aruba." The airline has told us to pick up the dog in her travel crate at the baggage claim area (though presumably not from the baggage carousel), which means we have to go through no security at all to enter that part of the terminal. We watch the monitor expectantly. The plane has landed. We wait. The passenger luggage is whirling around the roundabout. We wait. An employee walks past us with a travel kennel containing a baby bloodhound. He asks if we are waiting for a dog, too, and says he'll be right back. Very promptly, I must say, the same man comes out of the secret hallway near the baggage claim with a grin from ear to ear. He puts the crate down and tells my nine-year-old son, who has been waiting for this puppy all his life that he can't go near the crate or the dog until the head baggage guy has checked Mom and Dad's photo ID's, verified the breed and the breeders' names, and given his official okey-dokey. A few moments later, Aruba the puppy was ours.

The good news, compared to our children, is that this baby came pretty much house-trained with no need for diapers. This ball of cuteness didn't cry when I held her. We knew how and what to feed her and she did not pee on me as my daughter had done. Amazingly, though, I had to answer more questions and show more identification to take possession of my dog than of either of my kids. I guess it's because dogs are considered "property," and the airlines wouldn't want to be sued for giving the

42

dog to some odd individual who just happened to know it was "flying in" at 11 o'clock on a Friday night and decided to steal it. Of course, a human baby is only an actual human life. Who would make a fuss if the wrong person took them home? Who would be to blame if the baby went off with the wrong people?

Now, I have to say that once or twice for no more than a millisecond I may have recently wished someone else was raising my hormone-packed preteen, but her life is more valuable to me than anything else in all the world. You would think at the very least, they would have asked to see my license.

# 16. The Flu Is Living at Our House!

My eight-year-old son has been home from school with the flu for five days, and I have been home with him. I am uncertain as to how many bowls of chicken noodle soup and packs of saltine crackers I have lugged up the stairs to him while he watched the seventeenth episode in a row of some silly show on TV from the comfort of my husband's and my bed.

I have taken his temperature (he got up to 103 degrees) hundreds of times, wiped his brow with a cool cloth and fed him medicine he hates for the fever and the cough. I have also occasionally persuaded him to turn off the television and nap for a while.

My daughter got sick a few days later. So I ended up with these two small creatures who didn't feel well trying to keep themselves occupied while they healed. Occupying themselves inevitably involved arguing with each other. They argued about which game to play and who would go first approximately 6,732 times. They entered into physical combat over the remote control between 800-900 times daily. Meanwhile I was trying to write (I work at home) and they were driving me right out of my cotton-pickin' mind! The quarreling escalated as they regained health and energy. And there I was confined to the house while they were starting the third world war over who got more chicken soup, and blaming me when they didn't get enough noodles!

Seriously overwhelmed by my own case of "cabin fever" and sick of listening to it all, I got fed up with the whole mess and all three of us began grousing at each other, snapping and being extremely unpleasant to one another and to my poor innocent husband, who walked in the door after a day at work and got tackled by our son ("Daddy, Mommy yelled at us! That's mean!"), besieged by our daughter ("Daddy, know what Spencer did? He broke the rules and hit me and Mommy didn't do anything about it!"),

44

and me ("Honey, you're like two minutes late getting home! What's your problem? I'm stuck here with these two little monsters and you don't rush home early? I'm sick to death of all the whining and complaining going on around here. I've had it!")

My husband was shell-shocked, but when I finally looked directly at him, I re-alized there was something more -- he was sick, too. His face was a curious shade of green. He took off his coat, and said weakly, "I'll be upstairs."

*My husband was shell-shocked, but when I finally looked directly at him, I realized there was something more - he was sick, too. His face was a curious shade of green. He took off his coat, and said weakly, "I'll be upstairs."*

"I'm sorry you're sick. I'll make you some soup and bring it up later when I bring the kids' meals up."

"That'd be great. Thank you."

I heard my husband walk slowly up the stairs. Then there was silence. "Maybe... they're all asleep," I think hopefully. But not so fast...

The next thing I hear is my husband's voice, "I want to watch the news!"

Son: Da-a-d! I've only seen this episode sixteen times. Come on!"

Dad: "You've been watching TV all day, and I don't feel well. Can't I please watch the news?

Son: "I'm sicker than you are, I should get to choose."

Ugghh! With any luck, I'll have the flu tomorrow and somebody will have to take care of me!

45

# Middle Age

# 17. Just Received My AARP Card...

I just received my AARP card in the mail. I am not 50 yet. I will not be 50 for 109 days, 11 hours and 25 minutes. I counted. I mention this to my husband, and he tells me that he's pretty sure AARP offers people "the card" when they turn 49½, which happened to me two months ago. I am not pleased with this information, and I am in the middle of yelling at my husband that he must be wrong when I remember that humorist Dave Barry wrote a column about this some 10 years ago, and I laughed at the time because I was certain it would never happen to me! I sent copies of the piece to everyone I knew who was over 50 and felt smugly self-assured for several hours following.

Now, 10 years has passed and I will soon be turning 50. Truth be told, I am even retired, though not in the traditional sense. My cousin said it well, that at middle age she is "re-inventing herself." Nice concept. I have reinvented myself from one career into an entirely different career, and only the perspective of age and experience made that (very wise) transition possible.

> *I am not fifty yet. I will not be fifty for 109 days, 11 hours and 25 minutes.*

Still, I received my AARP card today, unsolicited. Someone who doesn't even know me, whom I have never even heard of, believes I am old enough to be a member of the American Association of Retired Persons. Keep in mind that this is an organization that my teenage friends and I used to call the "American Association of Really-old People." This was a group that my aging father liked so well, he never called it A. A. R. P. No, he felt so familiar that he used a nickname. He called it "arrrrrppp."

Please don't get me wrong. I actually think AARP is a terrific organization, and I look forward to the discounts and services they provide at a nominal fee. But do they have to include eye care (for my developing glaucoma and cataracts), long term care insurance (for when my children kick me out of my home and insist I need the "extra help") and a safe driving course (to remind me that I will soon become one of those ancient blue-haired old ladies behind the wheel of a car I have virtually forgotten how to drive)?

The letter enclosed with my card tells me that this organization would like to help me get the most out of life over 50 and I guess I should be grateful. Yes, I should be delighted this opportunity exists and I can read at least one monthly magazine that is aimed at me and not the 20- to 30-year-olds who are even now thinking they will never get this old. Yes, I think I should grow old gracefully, don't you? Still, maybe I'll call and see if "arrrppp" made a mistake...

...They didn't. Apparently 49½ is the new 50.

# 18. M.I.R.I.

I suffer from a disorder that no physician will yet find in the PDR (Physicians Desk Reference). It has not been granted full status as a disease by the U.S. Department of Health, but those of us who yield to its symptoms know this disorder is absolutely real and diagnosable.

I have named it M.I.R.I. (affectionately known as "mee-rie"), which stands for Middle-age Information Retrieval Impairment. Most of us over 40 or 45 have MIRI to one extent or another. There is the slightly affected individual who cannot remember the names of friends she bumps into on the street and hasn't seen in a while. Those of us who are profound-

*Another symptom of this dreaded malady is rushing out of one room into another as if on a mission, only to end up standing in the room you've just entered wondering what on earth you're doing there.*

ly affected by MIRI sometimes have trouble remembering our spouse's or children's names. In my house, this results in me calling the dog, whose name is Sophia (I think), this way: "Dave...I mean Grace...No, Spence...Sophia!" MIRI also causes things like looking for your glasses for 30 minutes only to realize they have been on top of your head the entire time! Another symptom of this dreaded malady is rushing out of one room into another as if on a mission, only to end up standing in the room you've just entered wondering what on earth you're doing there.

When I was first in love with my husband, I was pretty flaky and found my car keys in the refrigerator once because I was day-dreaming about my man. It was kinda fun and cute at the time. By now, however, the cuteness of being an airhead has worn off, and I am left helplessly abandoned to my inability to remember what someone just told me five minutes ago.

My children have recently discovered that my M.I.R.I. can be used to their advantage because they can convince me there are whole conversations I missed where I promised them all sorts of wonderful things. One example is when my daughter says, "Mom. Do you remember yesterday when you said it was okay for us to smear peanut butter all over the hamster to see if he likes it?"

"No, honey, I'm sorry, I do not remember that conversation, and I'm fairly certain I would never have agreed to such a thing." (Would I?)

"Well, you did, Mom," my son pipes in. "We were in the car, remember?"

(Obviously if it had happened, I would remember, wouldn't I?)

"I have no recollection of that conversation. Sorry."

"Does that mean we'll be in trouble now?

"Let's see. Did you smear the hamster with peanut butter?"

"We---lll. Yeah, " she says.

"But he licked most of it off himself," says he, "and the peanut butter smell in my room isn't quite as bad as it was last night. The hamster's acting kinda funny, though."

"The answer is "Yes, you are in trouble now."

49

"But Mo-ahm, you said it was okay."

"Yeah, you PROOOMISSED!" (Oh, this one always gets me)

Now, I know in my heart that I did not agree to any of this, but because of my memory impairment, I am not as confident as I'd like to be that I actually never took part in such a conversation. I suspect that I did not. I hope that I did not. But, these smarty pants kids are so believable reconstructing this fantasy dialog that I begin to question myself and can't bring myself to punish them because I'm really not sure what happened.

So here I sit, stuck with a peanut-buttery hamster, my glasses on my head, in a room I came into for a reason I no longer remember and while I am scrubbing the hamster with Head and Shoulders (after all, we use Pantene for the puppies), I try desperately to remember what the letters M.I.R.I. stand for!

P.S. It's "Middle-Age Information Retrieval Impairment"

# 19. Sleepless in February

Every February, like clockwork, I stop sleeping. Sometimes, it comes and goes every few nights over a two- or three-week period. Other times, I wake up on January 31 and simply don't sleep more than a very few hours at a time until I go to bed on March 1, sleep through the night and begin snoozing regularly again every night until the following February. I made no note at all of how Leap Year affected this pattern four years ago or eight years ago or 12 years ago. However, my guess is that I simply don't sleep well in any month that begins with "F," whether its days number 28 or 29.

> *Turning 50 is definitely impacting my psyche in good ways and bad, but it certainly gives me enough pause to be keeping me awake at night.*

This year, I slept every night until February 19. I have concluded that there is nothing I know of that makes that date significant except that it was precisely seven days before my birthday, and as I think I might have mentioned before, my upcoming birthday is one of some significance to me. Turning 50 is definitely impacting my psyche in good ways and bad, but it certainly gives me enough pause to be keeping me awake at night. Do you suppose I will begin sleeping again on February 27, when the day itself is past and gone, or will my traditional insomnia hang in through the very last moment of the very last day of the month? Will I recover quickly or spend weeks resurrecting myself from being "Sleepless in February?" Only time will tell.

The thing about losing sleep is not so much that I look like hell with deep, dark circles hanging down to my throat or even that I am more than moderately cranky with my family. Loss of sleep turns me into a person who remembers even less than I usually remember. I lose control over my thinking and coordination. For instance, in just one day, I have accidentally dropped two eggs on the floor, burned four pancakes while I was cleaning up the eggs and at 3:55 p.m. this afternoon, I hit a wrong key on the keyboard and deleted an article I had worked on for 10 days that was due in my editor's hands no later than 5 p.m.!

Yesterday, I was so out of it that I piled a bunch of clothes in the washing machine without giving a thought to my son's new red fleece pajamas. Yep, you guessed it, everything white, from my underwear to my daughter's new white knee socks is now a very pretty shade of pink! I helped my son with his homework and in-sisted that he was wrong when he added 2 and 3 and got 5! (Poor thing!) Worse yet, I was so sleepy by 9 p.m., that the Tooth Fairy left my daughter a $20 bill instead of two quarters for a stinkin' baby tooth!

I do not wear sleeplessness well.

I used to, though. When I was in college I could pull an all-nighter studying, stay awake enough to ace the exam and still have enough energy to go to a concert the following evening with-out so much as a power nap. When I was working on my Master's degree, I once stayed up for 48 hours straight writing papers and taking exams. After one regular night's sleep when the work was done, I was downright "chipper."

Then time passed, and age set in. Suddenly I was 40 with a little baby who hardly ever slept. I walked the floors in our old house for miles. I literally did the "baby bounce" for five or six hours at a time. She would finally fall asleep at dawn and be up giggling, raring to go by 7 a.m. I was a wreck, but I could pull myself together enough to shower and feed her breakfast before collapsing on the couch with one eye open keeping watch over the baby.

What I notice now, 10 years later, is that I have become completely incapable of functioning after losing a night of sleep. Whether I'm up all night with a sick kid or just suffering from insomnia, once I have lost a night's sleep, I am done-for for several days -- can't function in any remotely normal manner until I have made up every single moment of sleep I have lost, plus some! Then I begin falling asleep in strange and dangerous places - I catch a few winks standing up in the shower or more than a few winks soaking in the tub. I sit down to work at my computer and find I have fallen asleep while typing (this may explain some crazy prose every once in awhile). I don't fall asleep while I am driving a moving car, but I have occasionally caught myself dozing at a long red light. The other day I fell asleep in the chiropractor's waiting room and was awakened by strangers laughing at my snoring. Losing sleep is not good for my body or my spirit or my public image!

I have read that as we get older, we need less sleep, but I don't believe it. In fact, by the time I'm 70, I figure If I'm up all night for some reason, I will plan a week's rest in bed immediately following. Then at 80, I'll just plan to sleep more than I am awake and that should do it. And when I die, it better not be in February! Because I am taking the train to heaven and I have already reserved a sleeping car!

# 20. Laundry, Lunges and Laziness

I woke up this morning and realized that if I had made a New Year's resolution, this is just about the time I would be wracked with guilt about blowing it. I used to make a resolution every year, but after numerous failures, I gave it up. You know what I mean -- there was the year I quit smoking at midnight and had started again by 2:30 a.m., and the year I announced to anyone that would listen that I was going to start using that gym membership I bought six months before and had yet to use. I went and worked out like a fiend on January 2, 3 and 4 and never darkened the door of the place again. (This, by the way is how those places make a profit.)

> *I announced to anyone that would listen that I was going to start using that gym membership I bought six months before and had yet to use. I went and worked out like a fiend on January 2, 3 and 4 and never darkened the door of the place again.*

I hold expired membership cards to more weight loss/exercise programs, and have more free trials of weight loss products in my medicine cabinet than you can shake a carrot stick at, and yet I am still more than substantially overweight and out of shape. My mom would say that I just don't have enough "stick-to-it-iveness," which is a nice way of saying I'm a lazy bum.

The only comforting part of this situation is that so many other people seem to be in the same predicament. I have noticed in recent years that nearly every friend I have owns an exercise machine, treadmill or the like and in most cases, that expensive piece of workout equipment has become nothing more than an excellent place to hang laundry. I even have one friend who decorates the old treadmill in her family room for Christmas! With a little tinsel and some garlands, you hardly notice what it is, which, I suppose, is the point.

I have another friend who had her husband move the home gym into the laundry room for the specific purpose of hanging drying laundry on it, and other than sweaters with these weird handle-shaped sections, it actually works fairly well.

I find leaving the free weights in the family room is good because my son uses them to pose as a weight lifter to make us all laugh. They also make excellent, albeit large, paperweights. The ankle weights I bought at the sporting goods store (amazing they let people like me in) are now stabilizing the legs of a wobbly old table, and the exercise ball, I think, is hidden behind a large chair in the living room. I guess the problem isn't that the exercise stuff doesn't get used. It's that you have to be inventive in order to make certain you don't accidentally use it for its intended purpose.

Anyway, it is six weeks after New Year's and I am wearing a sweater with a handle bulge in it. I don't feel any guiltier than I feel the rest of the year. Our treadmill is still in pieces waiting to be reassembled after being moved into this house almost six years ago, but on the bright side, I am pretty sure I know where the exercise ball is if I should ever need it!

# 21. You Know You're Middle-Aged When...

**You Know You're Middle Aged When...**

...You see a friend after a long while and you end up spending some of your time together discussing the best medications for acid reflux.

...at New Year's dinner, you set your pills down beside your champagne glass so you won't forget to take them.

...your children, regardless of their age, sometimes look at you as if you're some sort of moron who was dropped into their life as punishment. (Oh, wait! That's when you're young. When you are middle-aged and old, they look at you that way ALL the time!)

...time to yourself means reading menopause guru, Christiane Northrup, and swallowing your hormone replacement pills.

...people stop telling you how great you look, and just ask about the dog and the kids.

*You Know You're Middle-Aged When... ...you tell a person under 25 your age and they look stunned that anyone could be that old and still walk under their own power.*

...you begin swearing at teenagers driving their parents' car and the car looks just like yours.

...your children begin ending your sentences for you as a matter of course.

...you not only look for your car keys in the fridge, but actually find them there!

...you tell a person under 25 your age and they look stunned that anyone could be that old and still walk under their own power.

... you vividly remember The Beatles when they were all alive, young and new to the world stage.

... people begin putting candles on your birthday cake one for each decade because one for each year won't fit anymore.

# 22. Never Do Today What You Can Put Off for 35 Years!

Two months ago, I decided that the cure for my natural leaning toward procrastination was to choose an entire week in the not too distant future, take a vacation from my usual tasks and devote the whole of the selected seven days to "cleaning up" all the loose ends in my life.

I chose the first week of May for my "Deal with Everything I Have Procrastinated About" week. I patted myself on the back for my ingenious plan. I began making a list of the projects I had to deal with. Promptly, I got heartburn. I put the list in a drawer so it wouldn't be sitting on the counter mocking me every time I walked by. This, I promised myself, would not impair my progress. I'd just have to make sure to get the list out of the drawer and write down a reminder every time I thought of something else I'd been putting off and wanted to get done during what I had begun to call my "procrastination catch-up week." That, and pop down a few Pepcid.

Unfortunately, but not surprisingly, putting the list in the drawer was just one more symptom of my apparently incurable case of "procrastination disorder."

*Some of you will be thoroughly disgusted with my lack of self-discipline, but far more of you, I suspect, will be relieved to hear that my week's hiatus to finish things has become only one more thing about which I am procrastinating.*

It gave me ample opportunity to practice the old adage, "out of sight, out of mind." I soon found myself feeling the relief of forgetting the things that

58

I most needed to accomplish. Which was exactly what I planned not to do!

Some of you will be thoroughly disgusted with my lack of self-discipline, but far more of you, I suspect, will be relieved to hear that my week's hiatus to finish things has become only one more thing about which I am procrastinating. Here I sit on the second of June. I not only haven't kept up my list, but I have not seen it since I put it out of sight. Sadder still, I have completely forgotten what drawer I put it in and have expended only minimal effort to find it.

I realize that the time has been lost. All my intentions were to do this before the kids got out of school, before our summer vacation. Now, I just can't take that week to catch up until at least September. No, that's a very busy month. Come to think of it, October and November are very busy too. And then, of course, come the holidays. Gee, I don't know, I may not be able to catch up on my procrastination until the first week in May... 2043. With any luck, I'll be dead by then and my kids will be stuck with the mess!

# 23. A Word to the Wise

My husband and I fancy ourselves fine gardeners -- although I have no idea why. I guess it's more a matter of we "wanna be" fine gardeners. When we were first married, my husband, full of new-gardener zeal, started tomato plants from seed. He prepared the pots carefully and planted the seeds inside in the early spring on exactly the right day. He gently tended them as they grew into sprouts and small plants. As he did, he dreamt of salads-to-brag-about with tomatoes fresh out of the garden, homemade marinara sauce and the like.

My husband lovingly eased the new plants into the outside atmosphere, just as all the magazines said to do – moving them first to a sunny window and then to the porch and eventually outside under a shade tree in

> *My husband and I fancy ourselves fine gardeners - although I have no idea why.*

their pots. Finally, almost ceremonially, he one day removed the seedlings from their pots and planted them in their sunshiny new home for the summer.

Enter ME.

After a week or so, the plants began to take hold and Dave wondered aloud just how long it might take to see small tomatoes appear. I responded that I had no idea, but that I had recently read somewhere that if you put some ashes from your grill on the soil around tomato plants, they will grow big and strong.

"Wow, COOL!" he exclaimed. "I think I'll try it!" And with that he rushed out to the grill, carefully gathered the ashes from previous barbeques and scattered them around his tomato plants.

The next morning, like an expectant child on Christmas morning, my husband went outside first thing to check his tomato plants. They were dead! Now, I don't mean they were wilting or even in the process of expiring. I mean DEAD-AS-A-DOORNAIL DEAD! Dead, as in shriveled up and lying on the ground, fully deceased with no chance of resurrection. Dave was devastated and I felt terrible for giving him this bad advice. What on earth could have happened?

Well, as we all know, seeds need to land in fertile soil, and after that they need love and attention, care and feeding and watering in order to grow. Problem is they need the right feeding and the right care. Sometimes, they even do benefit from ashes. Turns out, though, that what they do not need is ashes from pre-treated fast-lighting charcoal, which is filled with chemicals that poison poor defenseless plants. Maybe I should have thought that through a little better.

# 24. Ahhh! To Feel Young Again!

Some of us feel younger in the spring, when everything is new and the world and our lives often seem to be overflowing with possibilities. Others of us feel younger when we are deep in the throes of summer activity. Sometimes, my kids make me feel young again, but mostly, to be honest, my children make me feel older and more tired than my actual years would indicate. Just this weekend, though, I got bona fide justification to claim that I have recovered my lost youth.

> *Now you would think, wouldn't you, that a woman my age would have learned not to even dare think "How hard could it be?"*

There we stood, my husband and I, at the kids' Tae Kwon Do Picnic, watching the black belt demonstration, when the tone changed and the Grand Master of the school asked for volunteers from among the families to try breaking boards. He wanted individuals who had never done Tae Kwon Do before. Enthusiastically, I raised my hand, thinking #1, "What were the chances he'd pick me?" and #2, "How hard could it be?"

Now you would think, wouldn't you, that a woman my age would have learned not to even dare think "How hard could it be?" Every time I do, it turns out to be much, much, much more difficult than I have ever anticipated. However, thought it I did, and in an instant I was confronted with a black belt holding a board for me to break with what they call a "hammer fist." The five other virgin volunteers each broke their boards in four tries or fewer, but there I stood on my sixth attempt, no closer to splitting the board in half than I had been when I was eating my charbroiled burger at a picnic table just moments before. The Grand Master came over to coach me kindly, the eyes of the crowd were upon me, my children looked on laughing at me, my husband was watching me sympathetically, and when the woman holding my board inquired quietly, "Do you want to try a smaller board?"

"Yes! Please!" I whispered with the force of my deep gratitude and growing humiliation. Then, to my personal joy, the Grand Master called to one of his helpers, "Bring her a teenage board." My holder grabbed the new board, which to my mind was a much more reasonable size. I took the stance. I raised my fist. I focused on my target. The crowd yelled, "One!" "Two!" "Three!" and I struck that board, yelling as loudly as I could, and it broke easily beneath my powerful blow. The crowd cheered. My husband looked on with admiration; my son shrieked with pride and my daughter, bored with this meaningful moment in her mother's life, had headed off to play volleyball in a sandpit.

I have decided there are two ways to look at this momentous occasion: The first way is to acknowledge that I was too weak and out of shape to break a one and a half inch board with my fist.

The other way is to say to myself (and anyone else who will listen) that even though I am middle-aged, I use a "teenage" board for my Tae Kwon Do, thus proving that I am not really 50, I am actually 18.

I pick door number two.

# 25. A Teacher's Best Lesson

I remember many things about fourth grade. I remember having a crush on Tom, a handsome brown-haired boy with a magical smile who didn't notice I was alive, then or for the next eight years of school either! Just as nostalgically, though, I recall learning lots of wonderful things from an extraordinary teacher named Mrs. Church. I especially remember learning about science and the wider world. You see, Mrs. Church was absolutely crazy about science, and she got us all charged up about the weather and electricity and gravity and the world around us. Long before it was fashionable or even publicly considered, Mrs. Church talked about respecting the environment and saving the animals. She had a special passion for Africa. She taught us about its indigenous people and plants and its native animals. When Mrs. Church told a story about a tribe in Africa, you could feel the hot wind of the desert on your face. You could sense the ground shaking as an elephant herd ran past a half a mile away. You could almost hear the nearby giraffes munching on the leaves high up in the trees. You could feel the love she had for this place and its inhabitants. It was strange, too, because she had never been there. She taught and told the stories because being there for real was part of her dream for her life. It was who she was.

> *When Mrs. Church told a story about a tribe in Africa, you could feel the hot wind of the desert on your face. You could sense the ground shaking as an elephant herd ran past a half a mile away. You could almost hear the nearby giraffes munching on the leaves high up in the trees.*

64

No one was surprised, then, when that spring, she announced she was taking time off from teaching, packing up her and her husband's belongings and moving to Africa to spend a year (or longer) "on safari." Even at nine or ten years old, we managed to recognize collectively and individually that Mrs. Church was following her passion and living her dreams. In fact, I suspect we were as awed by that as the stories she told us about the trip she was already on in her heart. Our mothers helped us plan an incredible surprise send-off celebration for Mrs. Church, complete with our own drawings of images of the Serengeti based on her tales, and papier mache sculptures of giraffes and zebras and lions.

All these years later, I don't really recall that day as a "goodbye." What I remember is that we celebrated Mrs. Church's dream with her. I remember the damp gratitude in her eyes. Without even realizing it, we rejoiced with her that she was living her passion, and we knew deep in our hearts that she had taught us more by making that bold decision than she could ever have taught us by remaining where she was.

I don't know whatever happened to Mrs. Church or even how old she might be by now, but still and forever, I envision her in khaki shorts, safari hat and sunglasses, gazing out over the African plains and their animal inhabitants each sunrise, breathing deeply of her dream. Thank you, Mrs. Church.

# 26. The Toilet Paper Wars

My husband and I fight over toilet paper. We do, of course, argue about a great many other things, but the fascinating thing about this disagreement is that it exists in silence.

When I was in college, I spent a summer as a housekeeper and cook for a wealthy family who summered on an island just off New London, Connecticut. My "boss" and her husband were very particular about any number of things, but I was flabbergasted when one day she took me into the bathroom and explained to me that I had put the toilet paper on the holder incorrectly. I remember feeling very uncomfortable standing in the bathroom with her as she went on to teach me that toilet paper should always be placed on the roll so that the end hangs from the front of the roll. When I asked her why, she said she liked it that way because it was easier to use if she had just done her nails. If the paper could be accessed from the front, she didn't run the risk of bumping her freshly painted nails on the wall. (Wait... here's a thought – go to the bathroom before you do your nails.)

*I had never before met anyone who had given the proper positioning of the toilet paper roll this much thought and I wondered to myself if this was really the best use of her time.*

I had never before met anyone who had given the proper positioning of the toilet paper roll this much thought, and I wondered to myself if this was really the best use of her time. Clearly, however, this was important to her, and as her employee, I complied. The thing is, though, since that summer in 1977, I have not been able to bring myself to put the toilet paper roll on the holder in any other way.

If I lived alone, this would, of course, not be a problem, but I married a man who I later found out does not care which way the "TP" comes off the roll when he needs it, as long as it is available! In fact, he seems to actually prefer the down in back presentation, which, these many years later, still drives my control freak self to distraction.

So we argue. But we never say a word. I purchase the paper, put it away, get out a roll when needed and put it on the holder coming off in front. I am happy.

He uses the bathroom and takes the time to turn the roll around to his preferred position.

I use the bathroom again. And even though I rarely use nail polish, I am inexplicably irritated that if I did, the positioning of the roll would be all wrong! I turn it around. I am content.

This can go on for days at a time, until finally, the toilet paper and the tube vanish from the holder and one of us is left stranded needing TP no matter which way it is coming off the roll! I discover that my obsession with this slips into proper perspective as I search for the missing toilet paper and find it wet, rolled up and knotted around the base of the toilet because the kids were trying to see how strong it really is when it is wet! (They watch too darn much television) I steam as I clean it all up and when I go to get the paper towels, lo and behold, they are placed on their holder coming down the back. How dare he?!!!!

# 27. God and Menopause, An Eternal Question

Some women saunter into middle age like princesses finally taking the well-earned throne. They say things like "Oh, I've never had a hot flash!" and "Mood swings? They don't affect me much." I hate those women.

Others of us crash bumbling and sloppy into our middle years just as we've crashed through the rest of our lives.

Personally, I am more familiar with this way of doing things.

*How old was my mother when she went through menopause? How should I know? She couldn't even talk about sexuality long enough to tell me the facts of life.*

It all began when I was 38 and still thought of myself as a young, vibrant woman. Not a person in the world, including several doctors I checked with, believed me when I said I was having hot flashes. They said I was just too young, or did not have the profile of someone beginning menopause. How old was my mother when she went through menopause? How should I know? She couldn't even talk about sexuality long enough to tell me the facts of life. She hinted at them under duress, but actually talk about bodily functions? Not a chance!

So I went through several years believing that these deadly-feeling little flesh warming experiences were all in my head and not in my hormones.

But then the tables turned and every time I asked a question of my 35-year-old male doctor he would say, "Well, that is really something that has to do with being over forty." Suddenly everything was blamed on this arbitrary number – indigestion increased because I was over 40, aches and pains, loss of memory, migraine headaches – all attributed to my having passed this magical age, not the fact that I hardly exercised, ate too much and was almost always stressed out. And let us not forget the dentist who explained that the need for two root canals a couple of years ago undoubtedly had to do with my body losing things it once had in abundance.

Finally, by the time I was 45, doctors began sending me home with little black polyester "kits" of things that were supposed to help my health. I had jumped from the pink plastic container for my diaphragm – a remnant of my young, vital, sexy years – to a steel gray bag-type thing that holds a blood pressure monitor. I keep it next to the black case that holds my cholesterol-testing device. Next to that, there sits another personal sample of the passage of time, diabetes-testing kit and a jumbo, discount-sized tube of Premarin to keep me primed for those rare nights when I might actually want to have sex with my husband, who of course is three years younger than I am.

Now, I understand the need that younger people have to put us down as we age. What I do not understand is why God gets to be male and when he came to earth in human form, in my tradition he only lived to be 33 years old! My religion teaches me that God knows what it is to be human, but does God know what it is to be female? I have to wonder. If God does know what it is to be a woman, then God is just plain sadistic. If God doesn't, that gives us all the explanation we need for hairy lips, night sweats, wrinkles and urinary challenges as we age.

69

This is an actual spiritual dilemma for me, much like abortion and euthanasia. Where is God during a woman's middle age? The Bible has women giving birth in their old age (Sarah, 90, and Elizabeth, 88). Is that even reasonable? How can a baby feed on 90-year-old bosoms? How does a nearly 100-year-old chase a toddler around the desert all day? How does this relate to doctors who tell me that all my maladies are a result of being middle-aged and "middle-aged" being 40?

I'm not sure what the answer is to all these questions, but I have found something that makes me feel better – in my bathroom drawer, next to the Premarin tube, the blood pressure thing, the blood glucose thing and the cholesterol thing, I have set three sacred texts: The Holy Bible, The Wisdom of Menopause and The Joy of Sex (just in case).

# 28. Help! I Have a Chess Board on My Face!

All my life, on radio and TV and from other women, I have heard about "laugh lines," "crow's feet," and other tiny little lines that appear on our faces uninvited and most unwelcome as we grow older. But when I looked in the mirror a few years ago, I was horrified to discover that I wasn't just developing lines, but designs in the skin on my face. For a while I even thought one looked like an outline of the Virgin Mary screaming at little Jesus to stop talking already and tie his sandals! That one faded nicely with a little Oil of Olay.

Recently I've realized that the lines around my eyes have conspired together and formed a lattice type design just south of my "laugh lines." In fact, especially on the right side of my face, I am developing a full-fledged miniature chess/checkerboard. The lines cross perfectly and curve only slightly askew between my under-eye and the rise of my cheek. This is not anything they advertise solutions for. The "little line lotion" works okay on little lines, but doesn't even touch the game board on my face! The criss/cross pattern turns out to be an excellent place for my foundation make-up to settle in and stick together and just sit, not for 8 hours, not for 18 hours, but far beyond the promises of even the most reputable cosmetic companies. Worse yet, the creases creating this recreational formation on my face seem to deepen daily – last week I figured one of those little electric cars could drive through my wrinkles. This morning, now having taken on gargantuan proportions with the aid of my anxiety, my chessboard looks as if it could be a squared-off race course for an SUV! No little hybrid for me, but a giant, gas guzzling, politically incorrect recreational vehicle turned suburban necessity!

So, my question is this: Why didn't anybody ever tell me about the chessboard? I heard about wrinkles and fine lines, exfoliators and moisturizers, but no one ever told me I'd develop a game table on my face that could only be removed with the aid of the same sand blaster they used to clean my chimney last summer!

*So, my question is this: Why didn't anybody ever tell me about the chessboard? I heard about wrinkles and fine lines, exfoliators and moisturizers, but no one ever told me I'd develop a game table on my face that could only be removed with the aid of the same sand blaster they used to clean my chimney last summer!*

I have discovered a number of things like this my mother never told me. Things like hot flashes that begin when you're 35, a period that doesn't just stop at menopause but shows up again without warning every several months for years before it finally ceases for good. That everything on our bodies from head to toe, inside and out, will eventually dry up like a desert floor and that no mirages will ever bring back our libido.

Perhaps there was a pact between the women of my Mom's generation not to scare the hell out of their daughters. Yet, nothing is more terrifying than waking up one morning and without warning finding a chessboard on your face. Yikes, I just hope backgammon isn't next!

# 29. Lessons Learned at Middle Age: Part 1

Yes, even now, on the brink of 50, I am still growing. The ideas and pieces of wisdom that must have begun fermenting in me decades ago have finally begun to gain profound value like the deep, woody taste of well-aged wine. I write to you now from my proverbial wine cellar to share recent lessons that up to now had little meaning to my life.

> *Life is too short to spend it doing things that do not feed our spirits or nurture our souls.*

If it is not nurturing your soul, stop doing it! You know what I mean even if you don't think you do. For the years of my youth, I harbored the hope that my life was eternal, without end, limitless. This hope was so substantial to me that I lived as if there would always be another day to make a different choice, to live a different life, to fulfill every dream I'd ever dreamed. In my mid-forties, it suddenly dawned on me that my lifetime is not infinite. Someday, I will not wake up to a fresh new day. Someday, the choices I have now may be stolen from me by physical infirmity or dementia. Once I realized that, I also became acutely aware of all the things I had in my life and was doing with my life that "were no longer" or "had never" made my life or my character any richer. I resolved to waste no more time or energy on things or people in this category. I stopped writing letters to people who never wrote back. I began spending less time with people who didn't "get me" because they had never bothered to try. I decided that spending time with my young children was far more important than a tidy house; that doing things for and with my extended family because I was expected to was no longer what I wanted to do. I also realized, which I had never really "gotten" before, that I actually have a choice in these matters. If my career was no longer exciting me or fulfilling me, perhaps it was time for a new one. If I was "going through the motions" in some of my relationships while resenting feeling trapped in them, then it was time to find a better way. Life is too short to spend it doing things that do not feed our spirits or nurture our souls. My new middle-aged mantra is this: "If it doesn't nurture my soul, then I don't do it."

Life is short! And that's not bad news. If indeed life is short, then we just need to pay better attention. Make a list of the dreams you'd like to live for real before your life here is done. It's a heck of a lot more fun than sitting in your recliner bemoaning how quickly the children grew up and how retirement is rapidly approaching!

Live every day as if it is the first day of your life! ... NOT the last! For decades now, people have been telling us that the best way not to let your life pass you by is to look at each day as if it is the last chance you have to "get it right." I find that way of thinking extremely stress-producing. All that idea ever did for me was make me sad and set me to prematurely grieving my very own death. SILLY! A couple of YEARS ago, it dawned on me that it would be far more uplifting to wake up every morning and try my best to look at each day like it is the very first day I have ever been alive. That way, I look at every part of my life with amazement and appreciation. I am not so busy trying to get everything done before I die to stop and listen to my son tell me about the 20 different paper airplanes he made yesterday or for my daughter to share a secret with me. If every day is the first day, I can experience every moment as new and special.

# 30. Lessons Learned at Middle Age: Part 2

Find your passion and live it! A lot has been written recently about how you find your passion. In fact, many people go their whole lives long without ever knowing what their passion is. My definition is this: Your passion is the thing that when you do it, you feel happier and more alive than you feel doing anything else. Your passion is the thing you cannot imagine living your life without. When you are living your passion, you feel healthier and more energetic, stronger and more courageous.

I have come to believe that some people have just one passion that defines their lives, while others have different passions at different points in their lives. When I was a teen and in my early twenties, music was my passion. I could not imagine my life without singing and songwriting. Later, I was a minister and my faith and my ministry were my complete passion throughout my thirties and early forties. Now, as I have aged and grown, my passion is writing, so that's what I choose to do.

Too many of us get stuck in job or a whole career and wake up in the middle of the night 20, 30, 40 years later asking ourselves, "Why have I spent all my energy on this when I really wanted to do this other thing that makes me feel I am fulfilling a personal destiny?" Most folks decide to stick with what they know – that which is safe and predictable. But some of us have to break out and exercise our passion in order to live our lives fully. The main obstacle, I think, is that other people expect us to live the way we've always lived and have trouble allowing us the space to change in some pretty dramatic sorts of ways. Finding your passion is a huge step, but being courageous enough to embrace it is when the real life-giving shift happens.

Decide that who you are is more important than what you do. When I began my career in the ministry two decades ago, I made the mistake of believing that ministry defined who I was. I was not Gretchen the daughter or sister or friend. I was Gretchen the pastor, often to the exclusion of those other roles. In some

*What makes you who you are is your character, the values and standards and beliefs you hold to be true at the very core of your being. You are defined by your honesty, your self-control, the respect and compassion you show others.*

ways, that devotion to my calling made me a better, more faithful pastor, but it also had the end result of personally sucking me dry – successes in my ministry seemed very personal and fed my ego, but failures in churches felt like personal affronts rather than bumps in a career path, and over time, they ate me alive. I loved my work too much and identified too closely with my job, and it was not healthy for me or for the congregations I served.

Truth is, no job, not even a lifelong career, should define you. What makes you who you are is your character, the values and standards and beliefs you hold to be true at the very core of your being. You are defined by your honesty, your self-control, the respect and compassion you show others. You can be a fine, important, caring, contributing member of your community whether you run a mega-corporation, wait tables at the local restaurant or dig ditches for the city. What you do is how you earn money for you and your family. Who you are is between you and your God or you and your inner compass, by which you measure the worth of others and yourself. You are deeper and richer and fuller than what you do for a living, even if you love it.

What did you do today that made you proud? Not what did

*I have earned the respect of some very fine people in the congregations I served for 21 years. I like to think I have also earned the respect of my close friends, my husband and my children (although they may not admit it until they're all grown up). What I have discovered at this point in life is that that is enough.*

you do today to make somebody else proud, and not what you did today because you thought it would make somebody else proud, but what did you do today that made you feel happy to be you, that left you feeling lighter and better about who you are than you usually do, that left you with the sense of self-satisfaction that comes from being the person you always wanted to be. It'll be different for everyone. Last fall, my daughter earned her purple belt in Tae Kwon Do, and you could see the personal pride she felt when she receievd it from the Grand Master. In the summer, my son brought home a note from camp telling him what a good friend he is and how happy he makes the people around him. He smiled a huge smile when we said we were proud of him, but even better, he said, "I'm really proud of myself, too." As far as I can see, there is no better feeling in the world! We should each strive to have at least one moment just like that every day!

This morning I ran into a young man in his twenties who was anguishing over a failing love affair and a rotten job. He told me that when he was my age, he would probably look back on this time of his life and laugh. "No," I said, "you probably won't laugh. In fact you might even cry a little remembering, but that's okay because then you will have survived what's happening to you now." The conclusion I have reached is this: when you get older, you still have problems, and they seem just as big no matter

77

where you are on the journey. The problems are different when you're older, to be sure, but they can be just as disturbing, and the challenges can hurt just as much. When I was a kid, I thought my parents had it all together – that they could handle any challenge and weird unexpected turn of events because they knew something I didn't know yet. But now that I've arrived at middle age, I realize, to my despair and relief, that they were not any smarter or more capable than I am. No matter how young or old we are, we are simply human beings, and every day is filled with (usually unequal) portions of joy and fear and sadness.

Even if you don't think you've accomplished a lot in your life, you have!

Ministry was my first chosen profession 25 years ago. I envisioned myself as a highly respected, perhaps well-known preacher. I never became well known. My name is not a household word and I did not gain the respect of the world. However, I have earned the respect of some very fine people in the congregations I served for 21 years. I like to think I have also earned the respect of my close friends, my husband and my children (although they may not admit it until they're all grown up). What I have discovered at this point in life is that that is enough. I didn't need the fame, although the fortune might have been nice. I didn't need the popular acclaim of strangers. I need only the love and respect of those I love and respect, and that is more than sufficient to satisfy my spirit.

Sometimes, a lifetime of success is not always what we envision it to be in our youth. Getting your children to school in the morning properly fed, clean and equipped with the appointed notes, homework, water bottles and snacks and still smiling is as great a feat as brokering a multimillion dollar deal for a major corporation or running for President, and infinitely more fulfilling.

78

# The World Today

# 31. Automation Run Amok!

Not surprisingly, there is little written about the history of public restrooms in America, nor outside the USA, "comfort rooms" or "water closets." In my research I have discovered that "...architect Frank Lloyd Wright claimed to have 'invented the hung wall for the w.c. (easier to clean under)' when he designed the Larkin Administration Building in Buffalo, New York in 1904.'" (wikipedia.com)

Why, you may be wondering, would anyone research the history of public bathrooms? Obviously, it is not something I dreamed of doing as a young person, nor was it on my radar as I began easing into a writing career. However, I have always been fascinated by the level of angst public restrooms create in some people. When I was a kid, I remember my mom rushing into the stall before me, grabbing a pink plastic pouch type thing out of her purse and whisking out a tissue toilet seat cover to protect me from the ghastly communal germs on the toilet seat.

Growing up, we used to camp quite a bit. As anyone who has ever been camping knows, what passes for bathrooms in most campgrounds are dirty, grimy, sandy pits of refuse, often unequipped with toilet paper or soap. We didn't use the toilet seat covers there because there were no toilet seats. My mom wasn't worried about the gross griminess of the campground latrine, but stop at a rest area and out came the covers with careful instructions on their use!

I suppose this kind of concern is the root of the new "automated restroom" that we have all discovered in recent years in public facilities. First, somebody decided that flushing the toilet with our hand was icky, so they designed the automatic flusher. You know the one I mean, the hyperactive one that goes off the moment you walk into the stall as if acknowledging your very presence. Or the one that does what it's supposed to do and lets you take care of business and doesn't flush until you stand up, but is designed to flush extra furiously in order to keep the bowl clean, so when it flushes it sprays water all over the unprotected toilet seat for the next person to sit in. (Think what that does to those tissue toilet seat covers?)

I mean really, was it that hard to have an employee at the place run a toilet brush around those bowls two or three times a day? Apparently.

Then we moved on to automatic soap dispensers and water faucets. One restaurant our family goes to quite often has soap dispensers with a sensor, and you have to put your hand in exactly the right position at exactly the right angle in order to get the foam. Then you have to wave your hand under the faucet at just the right height to get a dribble of water unequal to the size of the lather now in your hand. The water stops. You wave your hand beneath the faucet again, but apparently, there is a time limit between the little releases of water. You have two choices – try to wipe the soap off with a dry towel from the auto dispenser (get to those in a minute) and live with the fragrance of orchid scented soap on your hands until you can a find regular old water faucet OR you can walk casually around the restroom looking at the tacky pictures on the wall or the tackier wallpaper on the wall until the faucet deigns to provide you with additional water to sufficiently rinse your hands.

At our favorite Mexican restaurant, the ladies room has a very interesting set-up; auto flusher that works well, but an automated sink, soap and water, which the manager and I have discovered, only works if you stand in front of the sink for a minute or so, step to the left and then step back. For some reason, the water will flow properly if you follow this simple rubric,

> *My stomach knots up, my hands tremble, my blood pressure rises. The "I owe money, I am a bad person" tape begins on an endless loop in my mind. What's stupid is that one of those collection letters can make me feel like that even if the bill has been paid and the company is wrong.*

but no one knows why.

In a restroom near York Beach in Maine, in one of the many lobster and clam shacks you find there, there is a tiny ladies room, which is very clean and pleasant. One afternoon after walking the beach together, we stopped in for lunch. My daughter, then age four, and I went to the restroom together. When we walked into the bathroom and past the automatic paper towel machine, it shot a towel out onto the floor. We giggled. We used the facilities. When we were done and had come out of the stalls, I leaned over to neaten her pants and tuck in her shirt and my more than ample rear-end hit the paper towel sensor and it shot out another towel. We washed our hands with actual faucets where you get to turn them on and off yourself. Before washing her hands, my daughter slung her sweatshirt over her shoulders, once more activating the towel sensor. More towels, more laughter. The water from my faucet came out hotter than I expected. I jumped back, once again falling in the line of the towel dispenser's sensor. More towels on the floor – hysterical laughter.

What a sight we must have been to my son and husband as we came roaring out of the ladies room in uncontrollable gales of laughter, our hands still damp because when we finally waved them in front of the sensor on purpose, nothing happened.

All this leads me to wonder about technology and how much of it we really truly need. I mean, how hard was it to go to the bath-

81

room, wipe yourself, flush the toilet and wash and dry your hands without help unless you are a toddler?

The other day I spoke with a company that had sent me a letter telling me my payment was late. I had already spoken to them about a mistake in the bill a week before and had been told that I should wait for the new invoice to be mailed to me and then pay it. When I phoned them to explain and ask why I had received a pre-collection notice, the young woman in customer service explained to me that these letters are "automatically generated" by the company's computer, and she added, "there's nothing we can do about it."

Now, I understand in theory that companies have, in an effort to increase their profits, automated a lot of their functions. But I grew up with parents who had major money issues, and I had my own period of trying to keep ahead of the bill collectors at the beginning of my adult life. "Dunn" notices, as they used to be called, make me cringe. My stomach knots up, my hands tremble, my blood pressure rises. The "I owe money, I am a bad person" tape begins on an endless loop in my mind. What's stupid is that one of those collection letters can make me feel like that even if the bill has been paid and the company is wrong. Silly, I know, but I am certain I am not alone!

So this stupid computer generates these crazy-making letters whether or not they're up-to-date and correct. No human input or intervention. Worse yet, the customer service people actually believe it when they say that the computer is in charge. Many have given up their control to machines, whether it's the Blackberry in their pocket, the towel dispenser in the restroom or the computer. Frankly, there are times when all three could go swirling down that toilet and I would be happy as could be to flush it with my own little hands!

# 32. Me and India: A Love Affair

Recently my children have been complaining about being bored a lot. Today, I got a chance to remember what it's like to be bored. I sat on the telephone with the same desperately helpful gentleman from India for four hours and 35 minutes. He was a computer tech trying to help me find the source of a computer virus we have contracted. Although I didn't lose any important stuff, the virus would let me work undisturbed for a few minutes and then without warning, suddenly begin bouncing windows around my monitor like it was shuffling playing cards (remember those?). This kind, but patently inept computer company employee tried the same things at least 17 times (and although there are times I am given to exaggeration, this is not one of those times) in order to rid my computer of the virus. Not surprisingly, it had no more effect the 17th time than the first. The only difference was that by this time, seventeen attempts were complete, and I had already wasted 3½ hours of my day. I was, not surprisingly, more than a little bit on edge – so on edge that even a nice dinner out with my husband and three Desert Pear Margaritas had little effect on my stress level. I know this because it is 4:48 a.m. and I am up fuming on my computer!

> *I was, not surprisingly, more than a little bit on edge. So on edge that even a nice dinner out with my husband and three Desert Pear Margaritas had little affect on my stress level. I know this because it is 4:48 AM and I am up fuming on my computer!*

A while back, I learned a saying that is applicable more often than one might think: "The definition of insanity is doing the same thing over and over again, yet expecting a different result." (Albert Einstein) We do it in medicine, business, interpersonal relationships and parenting. In fact, near as I can tell, everyone does it in some facet of their lives. And truly I don't mind if this customer service guy wants to have the exact same conversation with his wife about some stupid domestic disagreement every single day, but what is the point of having me sit on the telephone in front of a computer I own, yet am powerless to use, while he, half a world away, keeps trying the same solution to the same problem for the better part of my work day (and his), and keeps anticipating a different outcome?

By the end of the afternoon, the third phone call and the fraying of every possible nerve I possess, we were no closer to erasing the virus. However, he had added extensive new software to prevent this from happening again, even though now that it had happened, he couldn't stop it. And in the end, I had spent money I don't even have on more stuff to protect my already ailing computer from the illness it already has. And I bought additional memory to boot (no pun untended)!

Now who's the idiot here? Certainly not "india," which is the nickname by which I began to call him after our first two hours "as a couple." No, "india" and the company for which he works, contrary to all the pertinent evidence, are actually brilliant. I called them with a problem they had promised to fix promptly and efficiently if it ever happened, and they managed to make me feel like the virus was my fault, and not the responsibility of crazies out there somewhere who get a charge out of screwing up my life. And they got me to give them money on top of it all! And all this without the aid of any American citizen except me!

"India, my friend, I want a divorce!" Not from you. I know you were trying your best and in the end you were very kind. No, I want a divorce from companies like the one that made my computer, that prey on individuals in poor countries by employing them for a fraction of what they would have to pay you or me. I want a divorce from computer geeks and self-proclaimed internet gurus who make their living off convincing us all that we're stupid and inept. Fact is, I could have done what "india" did for four hours without spending a dime, but of course, if I had, I never would have made a new friend on the other side of the world.

# 33. Software and Pumpkin Pie

I am bewildered. I have noticed recently that machines are more polite than people. I can count on the ATM at my bank to inquire about my needs. It tells me that the reason it is not speaking to me is that it is busy doing what I asked it to do. It tells me that it is processing my transaction and asks me to "please wait" until it is done. It thanks me for using it. The fact is that it talks to me more, and more politely, than many spouses talk to each other!

Then there's the pump at the gas station. Of course, it doesn't apologize for the price of the gas I have to buy, but it does ask me nicely to swipe my card, complete with the "please" and "thank you" my parents so carefully taught. The pump gives me a choice of where to pay (swiping a card here or trudging into the little overpriced mini-mart while others wait impatiently in line behind my car honking their horns).

> *Then there's the pump at the gas station. Of course, it doesn't apologize for the price of the gas I have to buy, but it does ask me nicely to swipe my card, complete with the "please" and "thank you" my parents so carefully taught.*

It asks me very politely if I wish to receive a receipt – "No," I never keep track of my spending or "Yes," I never keep track of my spending, but with this receipt I could if I wanted to.

I even notice that my new microwave oven has the courtesy to speak to me. Even as my kids are screaming insistently and impolitely for food, my new microwave friend is wishing me "Good Day." I press a key that's marked "melt" and it asks me what I wish to melt. Press 1 for butter; 2 for chocolate chips (Mmm. That sounds good); or 3, for the crayons with which my kids decorated the new wallpaper. Once we have established that, it asks me how many of the item I am placing in the oven. After I tell it, it says. "Thank you. Please press start." The only thing it doesn't tell me is when I am defrosting chicken or pork and the oven has begun cooking, toughening and ruining the edges of the meat. Even so, based on courtesy alone, I would go out on a date with a good-looking microwave oven anytime.

This brings me to my cell phone, which quietly and courteously remains available to tell me what time it is. It keeps track of my calls. It says please and thank you. In fact, the only thing it doesn't say is excuse me when it rings with a call or an alarm at an inopportune time. Granted this is always my fault and not the phone's, but at the very least it should be programmed to say "Oops! Sorry about that."

When I boot up my computer each morning and go online, some unknown entity shows me a screen that says "Good Morning" and offers me options appropriate for the beginning of the day. Do I wish to catch up on the overnight news so I know who the U.S. is invading next? The weather is available for Tahiti, even if I live in Omaha. (I can dream, can't I?) I find to my delight that everything I left on the computer last night is right where I put it. No one has moved my works in progress like they shuffle the papers on my desk when they play computer games. My favorite sites are still stored where I stored them. The screen looks just the way I asked it to look. And furthermore, it uses all the polite words I ever knew – like please and thank you, excuse me, may I help, what do you need...

What all this tells me is that somewhere in the brain trust of electronics companies today, there are individuals who understand the importance of courtesy and know that polite interaction, even between people and machines, is important to our sense of well-being and happiness. So important that they spend years programming polite "human" interactions into the products they design.

My question is this: Where are those people when I am driving and somebody cuts me off in traffic while giving me the finger? Where is that courtesy when you and I come to the door at the same time and one of us charges right through it, leaving the door to slam in the other person's face?

My mom taught me that when I call someone else, I should always identify myself before I ask to speak with the person I am calling. When was the last time a stranger calling your house did that? When was the last time you did that?

A few months ago, new neighbors moved in across the street. As a gesture of welcome, I baked them a blueberry pie – I did it to be nice, to make them feel welcome and because it was the hospitable thing to do. A week or so later, the neighbors returned my pie plate filled with a freshly baked pumpkin pie. The man explained that he had been taught never to return an empty dish. This was his way of thanking us. We have an increasingly congenial relationship with these neighbors because we each went a little bit out of our way to be courteous and respectful and kind to each other.

Hmm. I wonder if I can teach my computer to bake?

# 34. Dinner at the Brown Derby

**S**ome people make a fool of themselves in front of one other person, while others just do foolish things that only they themselves know about. Then, there is me. I believe in doing things in a big way, so of course, when I made a fool of myself on our recent trip to Orlando, I did it in front of my family, our server, the rest of the wait staff, the hostess and the restaurant manager. Like I said, I like to do things in a big way!

It all started the night before the actual event, when I went for a swim in the hotel pool. I had to be ready to go out that evening, so I set the alarm on my cell phone to alert me when it was seven o'clock. However, when I got in the pool, the water was so cold that I pretty much got right out and went back to our room, forgetting of course, to turn off the alarm.

*I believe in doing things in a big way, so of course, when I made a fool of myself on our recent trip to Orlando, I did it in front of my family, our server, the rest of the wait staff, the hostess and the restaurant manager.*

We spent the next day at the Hollywood Movie Studios and arrived for our reservation to eat at the Brown Derby restaurant at 6:45 p.m. We were seated pretty quickly in a beautiful forties-esque dining room, which is said to be a 90% accurate facsimile of the famous Brown Derby restaurant where movie stars eat in the real Hollywood. The service was fantastic, the food was outstanding and the overall experience was quite wonderful. There was only one problem. At a booth just eight feet or so away from our table, there sat a couple in their sixties enjoying what we could see was a romantic supper together. The difficulty was a cell phone ring that every few minutes would go off from their booth. Clearly someone was trying to reach them and they were ignoring the call. My husband and kids couldn't have cared less, but I found the noise annoying and distracting and spent my entire meal resisting the temptation to walk over to their table and ask them to take care of their phone. So, I suffered in silence, but when our server came to our table to check on us, I asked her if indeed, that ringing was coming from the booth just across from us. She said she thought that's where it was coming from and yes, she could see how it would be annoying, but they were almost done with their meal.

Satisfied that I was not the only one who thought this was obnoxious and rude and highly irritating, I calmed down and focused on my steak. A few minutes later, my husband noted that the couple had left the restaurant but the cell phone ringing continued to happen every few minutes. Completely obsessed with the problem now, the waitress and I got up to see where the ring was coming from. Another waiter joined us, the manager and the hostess, and we sleuthed around the entryway and hostess stand like detectives in search of a clue. Until.. Suddenly... the hostess, less than half my age, says "You know what, the ringing is going where you are going."

"Yeah," the waitress says, "I think it might be you."

"That's impossible, my cell phone is in my purse at the table..." I reach into my pocket to discover that the annoying, exasperating, rude and obnoxious diner in the Brown Derby that night was ME!!!!!

I slink back to my seat, with my ego shattered, my pride in

itty bitty pieces, only to have to explain to my family that it was my own cell phone alarm I never turned off that had been disturbing the entire dining room since shortly after we sat down. My face was hot with humiliation as I watched the young waiters and waitresses gathered in a circle while the hostess regaled them with her story of my stupidity. No one has pointed and laughed at me like that since I tried to climb the ropes in elementary school gym class!

Not since "I Love Lucy" tried to meet William Holden has there been this kind of commotion at Brown Derby East or West. Still, Lucille Ball got paid to be that foolish, while I did it for free. Kindly, my family did not buy me the tee shirt we spotted in the Disney shop the next morning which depicted one of the seven dwarfs with this caption, "My name is Dopey. What's Your Excuse?"

# 35. A Car That Can Park Itself?

Lexus (aka Toyota) and other companies want to sell you a car that can park itself! And the options package that includes the "Parking Guidance System Package" and "Intuitive Parking Assist" ONLY costs between $5,300 and $11,760! Now, I don't enjoy parallel parking anymore than anyone else does, but I can't help but puzzle over why, when you are required to know how to parallel park to even qualify for a driver's license, any of us would shell out between $5,000 and $12,000 for the luxury of not doing so!

Now I don't fault these car companies for this engineering feat or trying to sell us on how great it would be to have. This is a free market and they have the right to sell whatever people will buy. And we know people will buy this, don't we? Probably enough people that the car company will make a lot of money on it. Good for them. They are in business to make money and selling us things we don't need has made more than one person very rich!

Still, I have to ask myself and all consumers, how is it that you and I can justify spending so much money on something we have been happily living without since 1901 when the first mass production of gasoline powered vehicles began? Get where you're going early and find a big parking space or park a little further away, get a space you can pull straight into and get a little exercise to boot! Or here's an idea, hop on the bus, hitch a ride with a friend, take a cab, walk!

OR buy a $70,000 dollar vehicle with a $12,000 option package that will let you parallel park hands-free to your heart's content. But remember this if you do - that $12,000 is 200 times the annual per capita gross domestic product of Barundi in 2007, and last year's GDP in Ethiopia would have to be multiplied one thousand times to pay for your $70,000 automobile.

*Still, I have to ask myself and all consumers, how is it that you and I can justify spending so much money on something we have been happily living without since 1901 . . .*

Is there any question that our priorities are out of whack here?

First of all, I will not pay more than $25,000 for a car unless it can discipline my children for me. I will not spend $3,000 for a washer and drier unless they fold the clothes and put them all away for me. And I hope most of us cannot spend money not to have to parallel park when there are families around the world who have never seen a Lexus, much less any car; parents who are watching their children die for lack of food, and children who watch their parents die before they learn to add and subtract, but don't have the money to give them a proper burial. And me, well my children are fed, my home is warm in the winter and cool in the summer, I have indoor plumbing and safe water to drink – I'm satisfied. And if I have to parallel park every once in a while using my own two hands and eyes, that is a sacrifice I am willing to make.

# 36. People Give Me the Finger a Lot and Other Things That Tick Me Off!

**THE RECEPTIONIST –**

"Your husband's kind of weird, isn't he?" The receptionist at my doctor's office greeted me with these words when I arrived for my appointment.

"Excuse me?"

"Your husband's kind of weird, right? ... I mean the way he answers the phone." as if I would know exactly what she meant. I did not. I looked puzzled.

"I just called and he said, 'Hello, this is the Switzers' residence.' It was just kinda strange."

"I know it may sound a little stuffy, but we had hoped it would help people pronounce our name correctly."

"REALLY??? It sounds so ODD." She paused for a moment, "Your husband's kind of weird, isn't he?"

Now, it seemed she was putting far too fine a point on my husband's level of weirdness! Indeed, I know my husband to be a little quirky, but no more than anybody else I know and the word "weird" to describe my relatively quiet, gentle life partner just doesn't fit. Meanwhile, I have to wonder, "Why does this woman keep calling my husband weird and obsessing over how he answers the phone?"

I am also wondering this: With a room full of people waiting to pay, make appointments and see the doctor, is critiquing my husband and his telephone manners really an appropriate use of her time?

## THE DRIVER (OR NOT) -

A driver is speeding past, through and around every other car on the street, honking her horn. Clearly, she is in a hurry. She does however, end up stuck with the rest of us at the traffic light, which has just turned red. She answers a call on her cell phone, and I can see her chatting from my spot right behind her in the line. The light turns green. She doesn't notice because she is talking on the phone. The light stays green and people begin to honk at her, but she doesn't move. Finally, I lay on my horn for an extended period of time. She turns around, gives me the finger and turns back around toward the steering wheel, presumably to drive her car forward to continue to her vital destination.

Instead, she continues to sit there chatting on her phone.

## SO, YOU WANT TO USE YOUR OWN DRIVEWAY? -

Years ago I lived in a very small Ohio town, where my house was located next to the only store in town. On busy afternoons, there were many cars parked along the street as people stopped to pick up a few things on their way home. I had been gone all day at a business meeting and was so happy and relieved when I drove into my little town, looking forward to a calm, restful evening not dealing with anybody else except my dog. As I approached my house, I could see that the usual busy-ness and crazy parking was taking place. Nothing seemed all that unusual until the fellow in front of me, whose car I didn't recognize, pulls into my driveway. I wait, thinking he is turning around and understanding that my drive was the only logical place to do so. Suddenly, I notice his lights go off and he and his whole family are piling out of their car and heading toward the market. I roll my window down, "Excuse me, that's my driveway and I am trying to get into it." The dad looks up at me, "That's your problem," he says, and continues to walk away from his car toward the market. I turned around and parked across the street where there were two or three suitable parking spots, and I waited...to get into my own driveway, to go into my own home, while he picked up a jug of milk. I waited five minutes. Ten minutes... 25 minutes later, the man and his family came out of the market carrying three cases of beer and a bundle of diapers. Seeing me waiting across the street as he came out of my driveway, he flips me "the bird." So glad we cleared that up!

## ROLE MODELS -

We have a parking problem at my children's school. The building was built back when almost everybody walked to school. The road was built before SUV's that take up two city blocks were being driven by stockbrokers and soccer moms to drop their kids off at school. There is simply not enough room for this many cars and this many children in one place. A little irritation among the parents is understandable - we are navigating a narrow street on which folks are trying to drive three abreast, while yelling at our kids and checking to make certain they got their breakfast off their faces! The aggravation is enormous.

One spring day, the situation reached a boiling point. Two dads had gotten out of their cars where their kids were still sitting and they were yelling at each other for being such stupid drivers. It was a quick and furious flareup and both got back into their vehicles in disgust, slamming their doors as hard as they could. As their children got out of the car to go into school, one dad leaned out his window, gave the finger, along with the accompanying expletive, to the other dad, who then sped away in a rage.

96

Just before school let out that afternoon, I went into the building to return a library book and happened to see that morning's offender standing in the hallway in an animated discussion with our principal and the man's 9- or 10- year-old son. It was quickly clear to me that the child had gotten in trouble for using inappropriate language on the playground. The father looked troubled and genuinely confused as he stared Mr. Jones desperately in the eye and exclaimed with exasperation, "I just don't know where Johnny gets it!"

*The father looked troubled and genuinely confused as he stared Mr. Jones desperately in the eye and exclaimed with exasperation, "I just don't know where Johnny gets it!"*

## PAY BACK -

A few years ago, I loaded up the car with trash early on a Saturday morning, and headed toward the dump. There was a line of 15 or more cars waiting to get into the town recycling/rubbish collection center.

I waited in line for nearly half an hour, slowly pulling my car forward a few inches every time the line moved the slightest bit. Finally, I am the next person in line to enter and a Buick Sedan comes up on my left and cuts into line ahead of me. Even docile Wisconsinites would have forgiven me for honking my horn at the guy, who immediately stuck his hand out of his open window, lowered it next to his car and stuck out "the" finger. I looked up to see that he was probably in his 70s as was the woman, obviously his wife, who sat in the passenger seat oblivious to her husband's passionate expression of his feelings.

97

A few weeks later, I preached the sermon at a local church while the regular pastor was away. As part of my sermon on courtesy, I relayed this story as an example of something that had happened in our own community. I noticed several uncomfortable people in the congregation as I spoke, but one older man in particular wouldn't look up the entire time I was speaking, and he noticeably shrank in his seat as I spoke. It never occurred to me why this might be until I was greeting people after the service. The man pushed his wife ahead of him and she and I shook hands. A moment later, he stepped forward red-faced to shake my hand and leaned to whisper in my ear, "Boy, I'll never do that again!!" Perhaps there is justice after all.

# 37. Too Strange To Be Real

I don't get it! What is the attraction of "reality TV?" It seems to me that life is already filled with so many crazy people and stupid situations that we wouldn't feel the need to watch even more of them in order to entertain ourselves. For instance, why is it that we (and yes, I include myself) will sit down in our living room for an hour or two on Tuesday evening and watch hopelessly tone-deaf, downright bizarre human beings trying to become our "American Idol?" Do these folks who try out truly expect that America is going to idolize them? Covered as they often are with body art, feathers, piercing and all manner of absurd costume and make-up, who is it that really even wants to make their acquaintance, much less listen to them obliterate some song we really love? And I can't remember the name, but there is this repeat contender on "America's Got Talent" who shows up in all manner of feather boas and sexy satin, which wouldn't be so bad except that he's got terrible legs and his only talent is calling the judges names that have to be bleeped, and crying whenever he doesn't get chosen. It's pathetic and depressing and makes me wonder aloud to my husband, "What on earth has become of humanity?"

> *. . . why is it that we (and yes, I include myself) will sit down in our living room for an hour or two on Tuesday evening and watch hopelessly tone-deaf, downright bizarre human beings trying to become our "American Idol." Do these folks who try out truly expect that America is going to idolize them?*

And tell me, don't we ever wonder why the "Bachelor" is a bachelor? Normally, the chosen candidate is supposedly reasonably well-off financially,

99

he is great looking, athletic, funny, charming. Doesn't this beg the question – beneath the surface, what exactly is wrong with this guy? Clearly, he must be an axe murderer that "goes postal" every time he sees a Dixie cup, or maybe for all the flash and smoothness, he just isn't a very nice person. Aren't we all suspicious that the man in question must have one hell of a character flaw or he would be married with seven kids by now?

And yet, enough of us keep watching that they keep making the show. Why is that, I wonder? Do we women imagine ourselves playing Cinderella to his Prince Charming or are we just fascinated by how all these spectacular, if not equally weird, women go about luring the Bachelor into their circle of possessive affection? I confess that I have gotten sucked into more than one series of the Bachelor/Bachelorette, and when I do, I spend most of the time muttering to myself at how mousy or pushy or ugly or snotty each of the candidates is. I sense within myself a flourish of superiority, which nourishes my ego. As the omnipotent judge and jury, I get to grind those men and women up into little pieces in the privacy of my own mind as they weep dramatically over losing a man with whom they have only shared five words. It's ridiculous, but it's why I keep watching and it may well be why you are watching, too.

As we watched Cinderella go by in her pumpkin coach with Prince "C" at Disney, it occurred to me that we may watch "The Bachelor" for another more primal reason, and that is that most women and men of today have been raised on the idea of "happily ever after;" the kiss of the sweet prince saving the tragic maiden; the idea that if only the right man or woman would come along, our life would be perfect. We would suddenly be out of debt, happy in our work and have the figure we've always dreamed of. If our prince would just get here already, we could be driving the "right" car and wearing the beautiful clothes all princesses dream of.

But the truth is that life is not nearly so neat or simple. Love rarely solves all our problems, and it certainly does not make us better singers or nicer to look at (although a little more love might do wonders for that guy on "America's Got Talent").

What it comes down to is that life is messy. Life is filled with more challenges than we can handle and keeping our heads above water is sometimes a losing battle. Perhaps we like watching reality television because it gives us a chance to say to ourselves, if only in the recesses of our own personal thought, "Now, there's someone who has it a lot worse than I do. At least I have the sense not to go on TV and make an idiot out of myself" or "I fell in love the old fashioned way, with a man who was dating only me, not 24 other gorgeous women. And even if he is not rich or princely, I love him just as much as any bachelorette ever loved her man!"

In some weird way, maybe these reality shows make us feel better about ourselves and our own lives. Perhaps watching these people on national television gives us a shot of reassurance that perhaps we're not so bad after all. And on the bright side, it might be nice to meet Donald Trump, but if I ever do, I'm not letting him humiliate me in front of millions of people!

# 38. Today's Television Commercials and Me

I am growing increasingly frustrated with television commercials these days. I understand that companies have to advertise to the market with the most buying power, but that market seems now to be defined as folks between 25 and 35 with a 30-second attention span. Everything about commercials seems to have changed from when I was younger – the music is now required to be loud and obnoxiously repetitive, the references to contemporary culture vague and the general portrayal of sex as a very public "event" is disturbing to me. Truth is that the only ads I see on TV these days that I fully understand are trying to sell me various treatments for my well-earned, if unwelcome wrinkles. And I would buy up all that I could afford if I just saw one ad where the woman modeling the cream or process was just a day or two over 23. OF COURSE, the wrinkle cream worked on her, she had no wrinkles to begin with!

And what about cars? Just once, can I see a half-naked MALE model draping himself all over the hood of an expensive sports car? I may be a woman, but I like cars, too. I actually manage to buy one for myself every few years, but I buy based on who and what can fit inside, not how many artificially buxom bimbos can massage it with various body parts in 30 seconds.

What about the concept of pharmaceutical companies advertising prescription drugs on TV and the Internet? I guess, I wouldn't mind, but I would much rather learn about these things from my physician or even better, my pharmacist. The requirement to tell me everything that can go wrong with a drug is okay in theory, but after I listen to comments like "This drug can rarely lead to coma and death." I generally conclude that I'd rather die

> *Truth is that the only ads I see on TV these days that I fully understand are trying to sell me various treatments for my well earned if unwelcome wrinkles.*

from natural causes than control my restless leg syndrome at the expense of my actual existence.

This brings me to my greatest pet peeve about commercials. I guess I am old fashioned, but do I have to listen to people discuss women's periods, men's erectile dysfunction and bladder control on TV every time I turn it on? Used to be that some subjects were sacrosanct, private, personal. Day was when no one would even ever say "menstruation" or pregnant on TV, but now it all seems to be fair game. How embarrassing is it to be sitting in a movie theatre on a date only to have Always pads or Viagra ads appear across the big screen? I've been married for the better part of 20 years and I still have to leave the room when those feminine products ads come on television. It's too embarrassing!

Nothing is sacred anymore, which is somewhat funny because we constantly complain about airline security and homeland protection invading our privacy, but we don't mind everyone seeing exactly how much liquid a "pad" can absorb while we're trying to watch the evening news!

I guess I just think that some things are better left to the imagination. Let's leave something as a mystery. I believe in the personal privacy involved in each individual's own hygiene and bodily functions. And even more, I never needed to have my four- and five-year-olds asking me what a hemorrhoid treatment was for when I was still too squeamish to tell them where babies came from!

We Baby Boomers are preparing for our retirement, so that someday, with our investment dividends, we'll have the same buying power as the current 30-year-olds, When we get there, we will buy up all the personal, private, gross stuff we don't want to hear about on TV anymore, and then they won't have to advertise it...

... until they invent the next personal, private, yucky thing they want so badly to sell at an outrageous profit to people who don't need it!

# 39. I Want Your Privacy Back!

I am confused. People have been grousing for years now about national security imposing itself on their privacy and yet... we will talk about anything and everything on our cell phones standing in line at the grocery store or the coffee shop. The other day at Starbucks, I heard a man apologizing to the woman he slept with the night before because he had forgotten to take his Viagra! Now, for me this falls into the category of too much information – personal information that should be kept confidential. I was suddenly bombarded by unbidden images of a strange woman in bed with this man who was failing to fulfill his sexual obligations. Eeew! Like I said, too much information! Especially before I've had my coffee!

Two weeks ago, I was standing in the cracker aisle at Stop and Shop, minding my own business, trying to decide between Triscuits and Wheat Thins, when this woman stops near me, answers her cell phone and proceeds to explain to her young son, in graphic detail, how to clean himself up after he'd had diarrhea. What I learned from listening to her conversation was that the nanny had refused to deal with anything "gross" (sorry, kid, that's childcare!). Now the first thing this woman in the store needs to do is go home. The second thing she needs to do is get a new nanny. Next, she needs to develop some respect for the people around her. Another woman joined us by the cracker shelves, listened for a moment and looked at me as she nodded toward the mother having this conversation and rolled her eyes. Meanwhile, I "looked on" and "listened in" dumbfounded that anyone might not recognize that this was bothersome to others. I spent years cleaning up small children and I am done now. I haven't the least bit of curiosity or concern about how this stranger's kid pooped all over his clothes and can't figure out what to do next while the nanny

> *Correct me if I'm wrong, but doesn't talking about your impotence in the middle of the coffee line kind of compromise your privacy, too?*

is apparently glued to her own cell phone. Go figure.

The thing is that some of these people who speak on their phones in public make no effort whatsoever to speak quietly or discreetly. They don't seem to care what anyone knows about them. They just let it all hang out there for everyone to hear. As a result, I now know more about the people who buy coffee with me in the morning than I know about most of the people in my very own family. It just isn't right!

What is especially puzzling to me is that according to my own calculations, many of these brazen cell phone talkers must also be some of the people who so strenuously object when their privacy is breached in any other way. They are the first to complain about the airport security detail checking their bags to ensure passenger safety. They launch lawsuits against companies who let their personal information get into outside hands. They complain about security in public venues preventing them (and others, by the way) from bringing a shotgun into the symphony or a switchblade onto a train because it compromises their right to privacy.

Correct me if I'm wrong, but doesn't talking about your impotence in the middle of the coffee line kind of compromise your privacy, too? Aren't we already obliterating those once clear lines between personal and public conversation when I stop at the toll booth to pay my toll and the young woman who takes my money grunts at me, and then says to a person on the other end of her phone, "Yes, and you know what? She doesn't want anyone to know, but she had an abortion last week." Doesn't want anyone to know? You just announced the event to a perfect stranger on the highway! It does not matter that I don't know the person she's discussing. It does not even matter that I'm not involved, but this is private, personal, sacred information! Frankly, overhearing it made me feel skanky, like an eavesdropper or a Peeping Tom. It felt wrong to have had access to this exceptionally private information.

If we are so protective of our privacy, then why are we so willing to have these very personal conversations out in public where others literally have no choice but to listen? Why do we worry ourselves sick about the safety of our Social Security number, and not think twice about discussing any number of intensely personal topics aloud in a crowd? I just had a thought, though. What if Viagra guy was sleeping with diarrhea lady? I guess they'd both get what they deserved!

# 40. We Now Interrupt Your Regular Programming to Bring You This Political Opinion

f your political sensibilities are easily offended, you may wish to skip this essay.

When asked whom she supports for president, our 10-year-old daughter, parroting her parents' views, claimed Barack Obama as her choice. When asked why, though, she expressed her own opinion in her own words, although her dad and I wouldn't beg to differ. She replied, "Because President Stupid-Head had his chance and he hasn't helped the orphans in Africa - all those little kids with no parents! And he started a war without a good, true reason. All kinds of people have been killed - Moms and Dads, children. 4,000 of our soldiers dead! He started it and he doesn't know how to stop it! Stupid-head had his chance - now it should be the other team's turn - I think Mr. Obama tells the truth and wants to keep any more people from getting killed."

When I was ten, I really hadn't a clue about politics - all I knew was that great leaders kept getting assassinated, but I couldn't understand why. I was five when John F. Kennedy died. We got two days off from kindergarten. I remember watching the funeral on a black and white television. I was ten when Martin Luther King, Jr. died. I remember wondering what anyone could have against this man who was so kind and loved his little children. Later on, when Bobby Kennedy was shot, I remember my mom coming into my room that morning looking shell-shocked. It was more than affection or even admiration for Kennedy - she had neither, but the look on her face told the story of a world that seemed to her to be spinning out of control. After everything she and her generation had endured through two world wars and Korea, evil finally seemed to be winning.

*. . . the look on her face told the story of a world that seemed to her to be spinning out of control.*

How much more keenly we can feel this sense 40 years later? The visionaries of those innocent mid-century years are gone. In fact, they were erased almost before they had a chance. While today, leaders who wage war without cause, and encourage divisions and hostility between different kinds of people get elected and re-elected. It just doesn't seem right. What better evidence of evil triumphant?

I agree with my daughter - Stupid-head has had his chance - now it should be the other team's turn.

# 41. Twisted

I am on my way to see my therapist today. There is nothing seriously wrong with me, but I do need medication to keep me on an "even keel." So once a month, whether I need to or not, I drop into Dr. Shrink's office for ten minutes, we sneer at each other with contempt (me, because I hate psychoanalytic types and he, because he doesn't seem quite sure about me.). Then he writes me a new prescription for my medication. The entire transaction on which my mental health theoretically depends takes maybe 20 minutes and costs hundreds of dollars.

The truth is that I am fearful that I remind him of that old Joni Mitchell song "Twisted":

*"My analyst told me that I was right of my head.*
*I said 'dear doctor, I think that it's you instead.'*
*He said, I was the type that was most inclined*
*when out of his sight to be out of my mind and*
*he thought I was nuts! No more 'ifs' or 'ands' or 'buts!'"*

The truth is that except for some bizarre and long-lasting hormonal fluctuations and a wee bit of clinical depression, I am as sane, if not saner, than your typical human - even your typical middle-aged woman! I do not dance around the living room naked with a bowl of oranges on top of my head. I do not dress up in weird outfits and walk around my hometown just to see how folks will react. It is true that there are days I cannot remember my dog's name, but with a little nudging I can usually come up with my own. My license number? I don't remember that. That's why it's written down on my license, so I don't have to bother. I have a healthy contempt for other Massachusetts' drivers and a decidedly minimal interest in technology unless it affects me directly and right this minute. So, basically, I am your average American woman.

I have a friend who calls medication at our age "better living through chemistry." Of course, she is well into her 60s now, so she may want to change that to "longer living through chemistry."

Her mom has been gone for years, and so has mine, but we each still talk to our mothers on a regular basis. I suspect we are much kinder to their spirits than we may have been when they were here "in the flesh," and besides, talking to them now gives us a chance to apologize for everything we said to hurt them when we were trying to break away and find our independence, whether we were 15 or 35. Mae and Dottie loved us in spite of ourselves, and my friend and I try to give our children the kind of love they gave us.

*It is true that there are days I cannot remember my dog's name, but with a little nudging I can usually come up with my own.*

I suspect that if I told my doctor I have been talking to my mother, who's been dead for 26 years, he might see the need for further medication, so I don't tell him. I also don't mention that I run through conversations in my head that I had with my dad from the time I was a kid until his death eight years ago. That is how I work things out with him still, because neither the Alzheimer's nor his death wiped away the pain he and I inflicted on one another practically from the moment I was born. I do understand that he is dead. I do understand that he cannot come back. I don't believe I will necessarily see him again in heaven, should either of us end up there, nor do I believe that it says anywhere in the Bible that I can expect that. Of far more consequence to me is the sanity of those who make up their own interpretations of sacred texts to

111

make themselves feel better about death or life. They, I believe, may be in greater need of medication than I.

So I saw my doctor today. Our visit had no particular tone to it and he, as usual, had little to say other than that ghastly therapeutic grunt someone teaches you in the higher levels of psychiatric/psychological training. He asked me a few questions and sent an email refilling my prescription. These analyst types are pretty clever really – they give you only just enough medication to get you through a short period of time, and then they require you attend and pay for an appointment to have the same prescription written again and again. The whole thing could take place on the telephone or in cyberspace, but that way they couldn't charge us for it. I wrote the doctor a check today, proving only that one of us is "twisted" and one of us isn't – I'll leave you, dear reader, to figure out which is which.

# 42. THUD!

can't even tell you which Major League baseball teams were playing, but it will be a long time before I forget the sight of a 40 or 50 year old man in a plain green sweatshirt leaping up from his seat to catch an errant ball. And catch it he did, to the joy and excitement of the entire stadium. So loud were the cheers that the fellow stood up again and held the baseball high in the air for everyone to see. Proudly, he waved it around until suddenly, in a moment I am certain he will relive for the rest of his life, the ball slipped from his grasp and dropped to the ground on the edge of the field with a THUD!

Who could not feel for this guy? Who among us has not made a stupid mistake in their lives, saying or doing the wrong thing? In just an instant, we human beings can go from utter pride and joy in ourselves to feeling like the dumbest person on the face of the earth. I don't know about you, but when I do something that stupid, I relive the moment endlessly, trying to make it turn out differently than it really did.

I fully expected we would see this clip once every newscast for a few days to come, but I never saw it again... anywhere. It occurs to me that it was just so difficult to watch that even the media couldn't punish all of us... or him with its repetition. For me, it was like looking at myself in a mirror and recalling every time I've ever let my pride run wild and done something stupid as a result. I would like to tell you that this guy's error made me

*In just an instant, we human beings can go from utter pride and joy in ourselves to feeling like the dumbest person on the face of the earth.*

113

feel better, that I walked away from seeing it comforted by the fact that I am not alone in making stupid mistakes. I had hoped that the reminder that stupidity strikes every human being once in a while would make me less hard on myself when I do it. Sad to say, seeing this man drop that ball and looking up to see the utter despair and foolish embarrassment on his face just made me feel nauseated. It reminded me that no matter how hard we try to be perfect and in control, we never really can be. It is the nature of humanity that we often make mistakes. All I can hope is that the next time I put my foot in my mouth or drop the proverbial ball, there will not be millions of people watching!

Here's hoping the same for you!

# 43. I Had a Nightmare That I was Sarah Palin (2008)

After watching the vice-presidential debate the other night, I had a nightmare that I had morphed into Sarah Palin. It was horrifying! There I stood, "caribou Barbie," in my excruciatingly repetitive glossy business suit in yet another color – (Maybe that's why John McCain thinks we women will vote for "interchangeable" candidates.)

I was the mother of five children, one of which was crying in the front row, another of which is soon going to give birth to my first, very public, very politically challenging grandchild. (Those long Alaskan nights and a good dose of abstinence education certainly did their family wonders.) Worse yet, I realized in those moments on stage with Joe Biden, that perhaps I should have "blinked" when John McCain asked me to run with him. Wonder of wonders, maybe the invitation to help run the United States of America should've overwhelmed me just enough for me to at least be humbled by the idea before I ran directly to thrilled. In my dream, I was Governor Palin, actually considering for the very first time the idea that running a town of 6,000 and a state of an only slightly larger population (whole state: 626,932 people)* might not actually qualify me to run one of the most powerful countries in the world. It hit me that as long as I approach every public event like

> *It hit me that as long as I approach every public event like it is the content and character question at a beauty pageant, they might just decide I don't really need actual experience to run a country . . .*

it is the content and character question at a beauty pageant, they might just decide I don't really need actual experience to run a country – as long as I smile sweetly and promise to allow a gun in every home. The worst of it, though, was hearing myself speaking in that faux-Midwestern whine, the origin of which even *Newsweek* couldn't adequately explain, although they did try.

I had a nightmare that I was Sarah Palin, but there were upsides: I was 44. I was skinny. And... I woke up.

*\* according to the 2000 U.S. Census, Alaska ranks 48th in state population. The only places with fewer people are Vermont, the District of Columbia and Wyoming.*

# Epilogue

My daughter just turned thirteen! You'll be hearing from me...

# About the Author

Gretchen Switzer is a 53-year-old mother of two who lives in Worcester Massachusetts with her husband of 20 years, her 13-year-old daughter, 11-year-old son and two dogs.

Both Switzer kids were born in South Korea and came home before turning a year old. Gretchen was 40 when they adopted their daughter.

Gretchen noticed that she was one of the oldest "Mommies" at the bus stop everyday. She had a choice between utter depression and finding fun in her situation. She chose to discover laughter wherever she could find it and the result is the book you now hold in your hands, *Menopausal Mommy and Other Essays: Wit and Wisdom for Women of Any Age.*

Gretchen has been an ordained United Church of Christ minister for 24 years. Her first book, co-authored with Linda Hilliard, was published in the fall of 2010. *Finishing With Grace: A Guide to Selling, Merging or Closing your Church* is a companion guide for congregations who find themselves having to make life-altering decisions about their church.

Gretchen welcomes your comments or questions via email at gretchenswitzer@gmail.com or please visit Gretchen on her website at www.gretchenswitzer.com.

CPSIA information can be obtained at www.ICGtesting.com
Printed in the USA
266586BV00006B/1/P